A SODA JERK GOES TO WAR

by
A.L. (Bud) Lindsey

A member of the
100th Infantry Division
in Europe during WWII

Back Cover Design
by
Ellen Fuller

Cover Photographns
by the Author

Printed in The United States

ISBN 0-925854-25-5

A.L. (Bud) Lindsey
P.O. Box 1398
Stanton, TX 79782
budreiux@lycos.com

Forward

For over fifty years I had pushed the events of WWII to the back of my mind until my sister asked one day if I wanted "those old letters." When I asked her "what old letters" she told of my mother saving all of the letters which I had written home during my two years in the army.

My family had lived in Brady, Texas, during the war and had moved to Brownwood, Texas, after I returned home. The letters in question were in an old trunk which I understood was my Dad's foot locker which he used in WWI and was located at my older sister's home in Brownwood.

On the next trip to Brownwood for a visit I was again reminded of the letters, so I picked them up as I left and brought them to Stanton where I deciphered my horrible left-handed writing.

Reading these letters began to bring back old memories, stored all of these years in my mind, some pleasant, some not so pleasant.

I felt I should put these letters in a form which could be easily read by my family and friends, and fill in with other events which I could recall after such a long time. This is the result.

...A.L. (Bud) Lindsey

The 100th Infantry Division went on line in early November of 1944 near Baccarat, France. The Division was near Stuttgart, Germany when the war ended in early May of 1945. Stalag VIIA, a German POW camp, was located at Moosburg, Germany, near Munich. Dachau, one of the German extermination and labor camps was located just northwest of Munich.

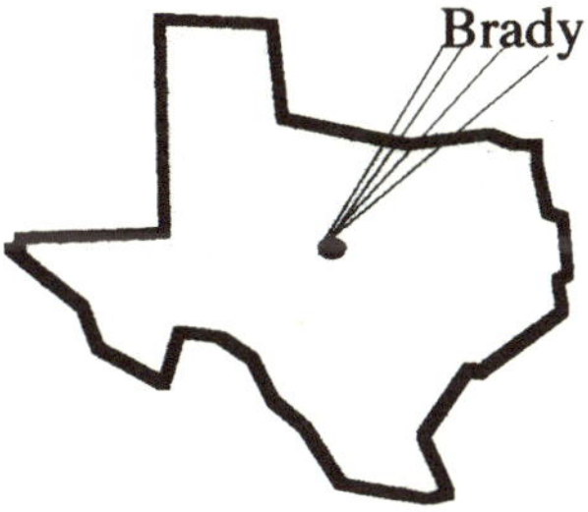

CHAPTER ONE

BRADY

DEEP IN THE HEART OF TEXAS

1941-1943

A SODA JERK GOES TO WAR

by A.L. (Bud) Lindsey

Brady, Texas is a small community of perhaps 5,000 located, some claim, in the exact geographical center of the state. However, with the state of Texas having such irregular borders the exact center of the state is difficult to determine, thus there are other "exact" centers of the state claimed elsewhere.

Brady was a quiet community, typical of small towns in Central Texas at that time. The local 250 watt radio station closed down at 1 PM each afternoon so the owner and one employee could go to lunch and have a siesta. The station then resumed broadcasting at 3 PM. On Sunday mornings the funnies were read over the air for the younger listeners or anyone else who happened to be listening. Also on Sunday mornings, services were broadcast from the First Baptist Church, the largest church in town. Sometimes funerals were broadcast of prominent citizens who had "passed over," the station's owner arbitrarily making the decision which citizen had reached a level of prominence to have his (or her) funeral aired.

The town's businesses, in 1941, were clustered around the courthouse square, Brady being the county seat of McCulloch County. It was an era when the rural residents came to town on Saturday and the businesses stayed open late. The local theaters had a one-cent day, usually on Tuesday, where two could gain admission to the show for the price of one admission plus one cent, a bargain of which I availed myself on the rare occasion I was able to persuade a member of the opposite sex to accompany me.

We high school students also took advantage of this movie bargain by skipping school on some Tuesday afternoons with two of us rebels getting in for the price of one plus one cent. We were alert on those clandestine Tuesday afternoons for E.J. Powell, the high school Principal, as he routinely made a search of the theater for errant students. We avoided detection by hiding under the darkened theater's seats until he departed.

The big event of the year in Brady, other than Thanksgiving and Christmas, was the Fourth of July Jubilee which was held, appropriately, on July 4th each year. There was always a traveling carnival in Richard's Park drawing a large crowd. The park also had a race track where the locals pitted their steeds against each other and out of town racers. Despite the fact that betting on horse races was illegal, some was present but not advertised.

There were six in our family; Dad, Mom, Dorothy Jean, myself, Betty and Mary Ellen. Being raised in a household where the males were a minority, did have some anxious moments for myself and Dad as often it was impossible to obtain entrance to the single bathroom. Dad, being the absolute head of the household, could just bang on the door and give an ultimatum to the female occupant with good results. I was ignored.

Actually, I suppose that Mother was the absolute head of the household as she in her quiet manner was consulted on any major decisions. She always had a good word to say about anyone and never a bad word crossed her lips. I can imagine her saying about Adolph Hitler, "Look, Mr. Hitler is playing catch with his dog. A person who likes dogs can't be all bad. It's hard to believe all of those bad things they are saying about him."

The depression was gradually fading into the past as the nation was embracing some of the new controversial programs from Washington offered by F.D.R.'s administration. One such program of which my Dad took advantage was the Federal Housing

Program (FHA). An FHA loan allowed Dad and Mother to purchase their first home, located at 1103 South China.. Always in the past we had lived in a rented home, paying about $10 per month in rent.

On the northwest corner of the courthouse square was located Cobb's Drug Store, the largest drug store in town where I operated the soda fountain, also the largest in town. I had worked at drug stores during my junior and senior years at Brady High School after school and weekends.

My first job in a drug store was one which was affiliated with Rexall. One of our most popular items was their product known as *Beef, Wine, and Iron Tonic.* Each year, or perhaps it was semi-annually, we had a one-cent sale where a customer could buy one Rexall item for the regular price then the second item of the same product could be purchased for one-cent. The *Beef, Wine, and Iron Tonic* was our best seller as the alcoholic content was high enough to make it very desirable in a dry county, surrounded by more dry counties.

A person living in Brady who was inclined to have a drink now and then had to travel a considerable distance to obtain any strong beverages. The Texas laws which allowed a doctor to prescribe hard liquor to be dispensed by a pharmacist were used routinely.

The Texas drug stores in dry counties, including the one in which I worked, did a brisk business with whiskey being poured up in bottles which had been prescribed for "consumption," snake bites or some other malady, real or imagined.

I was eager to take over the concession of the soda fountain from James King when he was drafted into the armed services early in 1943. Acquiring the fountain concession required me to buy his stock and equipment for about $600, a princely sum in 1942, which I borrowed from the local bank with my Dad co-signing the note. At seventeen I became a successful entrepreneur, dispensing ice cream, cold drinks, hamburgers and steaks.

The war had started and our nation was rapidly getting the armed forces built up to ultimately conquer the Axis powers. The busses containing soldiers and airmen in transit would stop on the square opposite the drug store and we would enjoy a rush of business. Also the bus station was located just down the block from the drug store and we were a convenient place for their passengers to obtain food and refreshment.

It was difficult to obtain sugar which we used to make "simple syrup" which we utilized "simple syrup" to sweeten such fountain drinks as limeades.

The Coke Cola liquid concentrate was very hard to obtain but we were able to obtain a generic brand which was not a well accepted by our customers as "the real thing." We managed as did most everyone else.

I was aware the war in Europe was in full swing with France being taken by the Germans and the battle of Britain was happening. But, for a 17 year old my biggest concern at the time was obtaining a date for the senior prom and passing Algebra II. Oh, I knew where France and German were located, but I wasn't too sure about the exact geographical location of Poland and a few other European countries.

When the Japanese bombed Pearl Harbor on December 7, 1941, it did not have the impact on me as it did older, more mature citizens.

There was never any question by myself or my peers of going to one of the Armed Force branches. We wished to go and as I was approaching my eighteenth birthday, I took tests to join the Air Force. The written tests were satisfactory but when I went out to Curtis Field, a local Air Force pilot training facility just north of Brady, to take the physical, I found, as I had suspected, I was red and green color blind. The Air Corps did not want me. I then took tests for an Army program known as the Army

Specialized Training Program (A.S.T.P.), a plan where after basic training, the Army would enroll the successful candidate in a college to study engineering. After this I merely waited. I graduated from Brady High School in the spring of 1942 and I received my draft notice late in November, 1943, after my eighteenth birthday which was October 1.

I was off to war!

CHAPTER TWO

IN THE ARMY NOW

So, I wrote home as did most of the young men caught up in the armed forces. It was the first time I had spent the night away from home without other family members being present. I, as most, was homesick.

Postmark San Antonio, Texas, Dec 15, 1943, 12:30 PM. A one-cent post card, not dated, but written at 8:25 PM, ASN 38,559,376, Barracks B, Ft. Sam Houston Reception Center

Darlinks Mater, Pater, etc, etc,

First night in army--boy, I'm enjoying myself. I thought you might need my temporary address.

(Pvt.) Bud

Our trip from Brady to Ft. Sam Houston, in San Antonio was by bus. We boarded the bus at the Greyhound bus station which was located down the block from the City Drug Store. Between the drug store and bus station was located Dad's Singer Sewing Machine store and a cafe operated by a fellow only slightly older than I. This cafe owner, whose name I have forgotten, was on the same bus to Ft. Sam and, as I, had been drafted. I carried a small overnight bag with a change of underwear, toothbrush and extra socks—no coat as the weather was great, as it can be, for the middle of December in Texas.

Unfortunately a Texas "blue" norther blew in after

our arrival in San Antonio and I almost froze my you-know-what off before I was issued Army clothing.

Postmark: San Antonio, December ?, 1943: 9:30 AM

#38-559-376; Co A; F.S.H Reception Center
Fort Sam Houston, Texas
To: 1103 S. China, Brady, Texas

Dearest Mom,

You all may refer to me as Pvt. Lindsey (spelled ey) as I am full fledged. We all got our uniforms, etc. today & I am extremely proud of them

Tomorrow we will all take exams and be interviewed, etc. We have a swell P.F.C. in charge of our group & we all stay in a good mood...this army is O.K.

Write me here if you have time as I will probably be here a week--just so you don't write too near the end of that time.

I'm enclosing a check for $15.00 that I wish you would cash for me & send me the money--take expense for broken car spring out first. Send M.O. or cash.

Will write again later when I have more time.

Love, Bud

It sounds as if I was broke, but only in cash flow. I actually had saved a reasonable amount of money (for 1940s) by working through high school and then having the soda fountain concession at the City Drug Store in Brady. Later at Ft. Bragg, in my stay in the Army, I filled out a personnel questionnaire stating the amount of money that I had made per month in civilian life. The company clerk looked me up and asked if I had been mistaken. I forget what that figure was, but it was like $100 per week, an unheard of weekly income at that time for a teenager, an income which was, unfortunately, of short duration.

I am completely blank about the car spring. Our family, like most recovering from the Great Depression, owned only one car. I must have had something to do with the broken spring.

Postmark: San Antonio, December 17, 1943; 9:30 AM

#38-559-376; Co A, F.S.H. Reception; Ft. Sam Houston, Tex;

To: 1103 S. China, Brady, Texas

Dearest People,

I'm still kicking O.K. We all took our classification tests & shots today. I'm going to be sent to the Signal Corps, by all probability--don't know for sure yet. I did pretty good on my exams.

I feel awfully good--good food & bunks. It was a little cold getting up at 5:30 this A.M. though.

I sent my tax paying clothes home today. I had to send the scarf & extra hankies too as the scarf is considered non- reg here & will have to check clothes when we are shipped out & extra hankies would be hard to explain, etc., etc.

Got to take shower Love, "Buck" (*possibly this refers to being a "buck" private???*)

We received all types of shots which resulted in some soreness of both arms. Along with the shots we received more than one physical. At first it was embarrassing to me to have to shed all of my clothes in a room of perhaps one hundred men similarly attired, waiting in line for a physical. I had been raised in a household of four females and two males, one of which was me, so I was accustomed to a level or privacy which was not offered nor attained in the Army.

We were interviewed, shot, and reshot, sometimes running a gauntlet consisting of two medics, one or more on each side, giving us shots in both arms. We were interviewed by an officer who wished to know if I had any girl friends. I thought it rather an absurd question line, but I answered truthfully that I did indeed have one or more girl friends, and I looked forward to the problems which arose when juggling late dates, early dates and dates in between if available. It was not until a few years later that I realized the reason for the questions.

I really don't know why I thought I might be assigned to the Signal Corps as one of the tests given, among many, was a test for my talent to receive the Morse code. We were seated at a long table and listened to a message in the Morse code. The only Morse code that I knew was for "SOS." I had no idea of the content of the message even though as a teenager I was very interested in electronics, ordering items such as crystal radio parts from Allied Radio, an early electronics mail order supply firm.

Postmark: San Antonio, December 23, 1943, 9:30 AM

#38-559-376; Co. A; F.S.H. Recp. Center; Ft. Sam Houston, Texas

Dear Mom,

They're still keeping us pretty busy & still we just piddle around. Some of the work is pretty tough though---for instance tomorrow I go on K.P, again (my second phase at that type of manual labor). This evening & morning I was a guard replacement for a G.I. who had to take an Air Corps test. I went over to the Guard House at 8 AM & slept until chow time about 11:00 AM. I walked guard around some storage lumber for two hours and then went back to loafing.

Day before yesterday I was a runner at the examination station showing incoming civilians around.

I ran across an old boy that I used to know in Alice here who had just come in a day or two behind me---John Henderson. I didn't know him very well but it was nice to see him.

A few of the boys that came down from Brady with us (about 4 or 5) are being shipped out in the morning! They naturally don't know where to. It looks like we will wait until after Xmas to ship---hope so. If you all would hurry up and send that money that I wrote a check for I might get to come home if I can chisel the Sergeant out of a two day pass. Have something good for Xmas dinner.

Did Dad crate up that scooter yet? Just wondered, no hurry about it.

It's 8:00 guess I'd better crawl under a G.I. blanket---have to get up early in the morning.

Bud

(*Note added to last of this letter in Mother's handwriting: "We cashed his check and sent a money order a week ago this A.M.(Sat.) and he hadn't recd it--so I wired him 10.00 yesterday eve. but when he phoned he had finally recd the M.O. but not the wire. Then he didn't get the pass. Such is life")*

Walking guard was a problem for me at first. If I had to walk my shift immediately after eating, I would get sick. It took some time before my system was used to the Army food and routine. It also seemed pretty silly to have a guard walking around a pile of lumber which was secured inside an Army post and the chance of the lumber being stolen was slim. Besides, we did not have a rifle to carry, and if we did, we had no ammunition.

When I was in high school I owned two motor scooters, one a Cushman and the other being some odd brand. Having two was very nice as I could work on one while riding the other. Rarely was the time when both were inoperative. Naturally our family owned only one automobile, a 1936 Ford four-door sedan, the availability of which was subject to negotiations each time I wanted to go on a date. Courting a young lady on a Cushman motor scooter has its limitations.

The reference to crating the motor scooter was because my cousin, Alex Houston, who lived near Houston wanted to purchase it as I was being drafted. It had to be crated so the motor freight company would accept it for shipment. I do not remember the final price I received for the scooter nor do I remember what the cost of shipping the crated scooter from Brady to Houston. The story I received later from Alex was he uncrated the scooter at the freight terminal, fired it up and it almost caused a big wreck as he did not know where the brakes were located.

No postmark...envelope missing. Letter dated Dec 25, 43, 9:00 AM. From Fort Sam Houston Reception Center.

Dearest Mom,

I looked forward to coming home last night but when the passes were handed out I wasn't among the lucky ones. Some of the boys who came down with us, Shipman, Turner, Shafer, A.C. Doyle, all got passes but they evidently didn't want to let a valuable man like myself out of the post for fear something would happen that would need my attention, no?

We went on a 5 or 8 mile hike yesterday morning & didn't do anything yesterday afternoon. I was feeling pretty low last night & the corporal wanted a

runner up at the telegraph receiving station. I went up and helped a couple of corporals there until almost 10 PM & worked myself out of a morbid state of mind.
The menu on the back if you will observe helps also, no? *(the letter had the Christmas dinner menu on the back)* Also we haven't anything to do this morning or probably this evening. I'll see if I can get a pass this evening & go to town to the show.

Thanks for the M.O.--what happened to the rest of the $20.00--tax or cost of handling & mailing?

We are still here but will be shipped out probably this coming week--if not I'll have an excellent chance to be home New Years--I think!

Tell Mary Ellen that I'd like to see her in that evening dress & can hardly wait to taste the fruit cake if I get to--will I?

Love ya, Bud

Postmark Columbus, N. Mex. Dec 30, 1943. This was a Christmas card, unsigned, addressed to 1103 South China, Brady, Texas, which I had dropped out the window of the troop train to a group of children who were waving at the soldiers when it stopped in Columbus, NM, in transit to California. It did not have a return address, but was marked "free,"and was honored by the post office and delivered to Brady.

If a G.I. wished his mail to go Air Mail, he had to purchase a stamp. But, if it was for regular mail he merely marked "free" in the area of the envelope where a stamp would have normally been placed.

Sending mail home by air mail called for some thought as the Air Mail stamp cost a whopping 8¢ which, if you wrote enough letters by this carrier, took a large dent in the $50 per month's salary which a private in the Army received.

The train trip to California from San Antonio took some time and we were fortunate to be riding in a Pullman sleeping car. We had a layover in the railroad switching yards at Big Spring, Texas, a West Texas town where our family had lived in 1936.

The trip west was during the daylight hours and I had the chance to see coyotes, antelope and other wildlife. It was a new adventure for a young lad who had never been anywhere to speak of. After our troop train arrived in California it was routed to a siding where we waited to allow other train traffic to clear. This stop just happened to be beside an orange grove and the temptation proved too great for many of the inductees as they departed the train to pick a few oranges.

Dear Mom & Pop,

I'm out in California--Camp Roberts about 250 miles northeast of Los Angeles. I haven't been given an address as yet as we may be moved this evening.

I know for certain that I'm in the infantry & according to what they say, I'll stay in the infantry--

dern it & I wanted in the Signal Crops.

We'll be here about seventeen weeks for our basic training.

It's a pretty swell camp but not as modern as Ft. Sam--for instance the barracks are not as warm as at Ft. Sam & I also can't find a plug to use my electric razor here.

It's a pretty big place--it'll take a three day pass for me to find the gate. There are hills all around & it's pretty country. We came through about 6 tunnels coming from L.A. on the train.

I mailed you all a letter from Columbus, N.M. the other day--did you get it?

I sent in my A.S.T.P. papers & maybe I will get to go to college.

I'm sending you a check for $20.00--Ten of it for that money order that you sent me Xmas & ten for another money order that I want you to send me as soon as I get my address; which will be about tomorrow. That is, I'll write again tomorrow. I'll need some money for a hat & maybe another field jacket.

Also I wish you'd revise that box that I packed for you to send me & get it almost ready to go! Don't close it yet as I may need a few other things.

I want my:

35 mm Argus Camera (that's my little new one)

This would have been an Argus C-3 camera which was a good choice of a camera for that time. The price in 1942-43 would have been about $40. A lesser camera would have been a Kodak which did not use 35mm film. If a person wished a better camera it would have been a Leica, much more expensive. The $40 was a lot of money; however, I doubt that I purchased the camera new, but settled for a used model. I lost this Argus C-3 camera in France somewhere..it was in my duffel bag which was lost in the confusion of the war. The letter continues...

Two boxes of 35mm film; one box isn't even opened—it's a little sq box about 2" X 4"& the other is a little bigger—be careful not to unseal them & expose them to light—both are in the cartons that were mailed to me & still have the film company's return address on them. Send me my box of color film (135) (Kodak) My buckskin house slippers--I'm going to buy myself a pair of civilian tan shoes. About three or four handkerchiefs & that wool scarf if Dad doesn't mind.

I'm sending you a menu of our New Year's day dinner. It was good but I haven't found anything that will compare to what you used to have. I'll be home to eat one of those home cooked meals in seventeen weeks--in May. Maybe I can go down to Betty's graduation & Tommy's if he ever makes it. The war will be over by the time Polly gets out, no?

Happy New Year, Bud

Camp Roberts, Calif; Postmark Jan 10, 1944

Jan 5, (Wednesday) 1944; #38-559-376; Co. B; 90 Inf. Training Bn, Platoon 3

Dear Mater & Pater,

I'm still kicking-but a little slower. This is the first time that I've had off since Sunday. The C.O. had a program worked out for us that is air tight. We went on an 8 mile hike last night with light combat pack.

We'll probably go on one in a day or two with full pack...Ugh!

Also we've been seeing special training motion pictures, etc--learning our manual of arms & drill. Uncle Sam is spending a lot of money on us.

I got a letter from you, Mom & Homer's Xmas card, too this evening, thanks.

Thurs...There's a rumor going around camp that we're going on another hike (10 m.) tonight with full pack. The weather is warm--not warm enough. I thought that this state was known as sunny Calif. There's fog almost every morning & then it usually rains in the evening & clears off at night.

Friday...

Saturday...Was called out so missed Friday altogether---you see they do keep us pretty busy.

We did go on that hike Thurs. night, but only went 2 miles & practiced throwing up dispersed pup tents & came on back. I surely was tired. We all went up on a hill that is just west of our barracks this morning & practiced some more.

My A.S.T.P. papers came through and I'm being shipped at 4:30 this evening---Georgia (Ft. Benning) I'm almost certain. It's 2:30 now so I'll have to go ahead & send this messy letter (i.e., first page) as I have a lot of other things to do also. I don't know how or how many are going---wish I was going alone. I'd come through Brady & miss connections, yes?

Mom, you go on & write me whether you have anything to say or not. I look forward to your letters an awfully lot. I haven't had time to write much to anyone else--got a letter from Harry (*Shannon*)--Homer & Jack. Tell Tommy, Alvie & Virginia that I'll write them as soon as I have time.

All my clothes are dirty & have been afraid to send them to the laundry or wash them out myself for fear that they would ship me out. I went over to the clothing P.X. for a few minutes last night & bought me a pair of G.I. long-handles (olive drab). They cost me $3.50 but are the best & warmest that I've ever had (wool).

My mail will reach me OK so go ahead & send it here.

Love, Bud

One of the problems which I encountered with the army training was getting the army-issue boots broke in. They were two or three times as heavy as the civilian shoes which I had been accustomed and my knees and legs suffered for a period of time. I think all shoes or boots in 1943 required a "breaking in" period, unlike our modern footwear.

Also the helmets issued to the troops were hard to get used to. They were heavy, heavier than any type of headgear I had ever worn and it took some time for my neck muscles to accept this new load.

Post mark El Paso, Jan 11, 1944, 8:30 AM

Pvt. A. Lindsey; 90 Inf Tran Btn; Co B, 3rd Platoon; Camp Roberts

Dear Mom (Mater),

We're on our way finally. It seems that the old army slogan of "Hurry up & wait" still holds true.

We've been piddling around. Think it will be no doubt for the next 4 or 5 days. I'll get to come back through Texas (S.A.) again anyway

How's the old household running? Tell the girls to write me. I want to hear from all three. All donations along that line will be appreciated by this G.I.

This trip will give me a chance to rest up & write some letters. I don't know any of the fellow "inmates." There are only a few A.S.T.P. recruits along. The rest are a different bunch.

We had a layover in Los Angeles this morning from about 8:00 AM until 3 PM--naturally I stayed in the coach & read magazines, Ha! I ran around a while bought a service cap (with blue Inf. braid on it...I'll be a good looking soldier after my hair grows out sufficiently to groom & I'm issued my "brass" insignias & maybe qualify for rifle metals, etc.) Then took in a double feature, intermittently gazing with profound fascination at the display of ankles & sights, etc. etc.

I hated to leave the camp--we had some awfully nice officers. Our platoon leader, 2nd Lt. Holloway, was young and tough. He would cuss us all out while we were all drilling then joke with us during our breaks. Most of us were from Texas- so was he, so we considered the 3rd platoon as the best in the co. ("The rough & rugged Texans" we were known as)

We had a former barber in the 1st squad of our platoon & Sat afternoon he set up his barber shop in the latrine (next room to ours) & did a rushing business. One big old dumb country boy kept telling him to take more off of the top so he scalped him-he surely did look funny.

Mom, bundle up those two volumes of "Practical Mathematics" & any loose issues of the same ready for mailing. When I send you my next address & ask for them. I really want them in a hurry. Also I think I'll need my slide rule. I think that it is in that cardboard box that I packed in the wash house. It's in a leather cover. I'll need to brush up on my Algebra in order to make the grade. I'm not in the A.S.T.P. as yet,

Love Bud

One trip which I made—perhaps it was this one between L.A. and Fort Benning—there were about six of us traveling with a Sergeant in charge who was responsible to see to our well being and be sure we got to our destination. Part of the Sergeant's duty was to arrange for our meals. I remember we stopped at one restaurant and we were all served a plate lunch, all with the same entree — chicken pot pie. Not having been anywhere much (one person once asked of me, "You ain't been much, have you?"), I had never heard of chicken pot pie. Fried chicken, yes, but not chicken pot pie. I thought it was a special dessert made with chicken and ate all the lunch, saving what I thought was the dessert (chicken pot pie) until last. I was not alone. I suppose if it hadn't been for WWII we would have never tasted pizza, avocado or chow mien, and our diet would have stayed hamburgers, chicken fried steak, okra, blackeyed peas, cornbread, and sweet milk.

CHAPTER THREE

ASTP BASIC TRAINING

FORT BENNING, GEORGIA

Postmark; Fort Benning, Georgia; Jan 15, 1944; Pvt. A. Lindsey; ASN38,559,376; 2nd Company; 5th Regiment; A.S.T.P.; B.T.C.

Dearest Mater,

We finally got off that train—wish I had stayed on! The living accommodations aren't as good as could be. The weather is sloppy & wet and the chow isn't as good--no doubt I'll live.

We haven't done anything as yet-it looks like I'm in-I had my doubts before. The way they (the noncoms) talk chances for flunking are rather small compared to my previous assumption.

We have pine trees all around the place & have coal heaters in our huts (they should have called them shacks) which are tar paper.We have a bunch of Italian prisoners here-they roam around just like we do-free almost. There's a bunch of boys talking to about three of the POWs out front now. The POWs carry a little dictionary around & they can converse with us a little--we're not supposed to talk to them though.

Send me that money order for $10.00 if it doesn't inconvenience you all too much If you will recall I sent you a $20 check to cover that $10 that you sent me Xmas. I got a partial pay first as I left Camp Roberts but I had to buy some underwear, socks, handkerchiefs, etc.--no gambling as yet. Also send me my two cameras <u>and flash attachment</u> (the flash attachment is in that big trunk with my other photography equipment) Also all of the film. How about sending me two or three pairs of briefs & two or three or four of those sweat shirts (white or any color) that I have in the clothing trunk (scarf, too). I'd like to have those math books too (ship the slide rule) & "Elements of Radio"--I probably won't have much time to study but I'll try. If all of this parcel post rate runs up I'll pay you all for it--send those long handles (red) of mine also--I'll be a company attraction! Ha! I'd like that writing kit too that Jean gave me.

We laid over in Birmingham, Ala., yesterday for about 8 hours. I went to a couple of shows & ran around admiring the southern feminine population, etc.

Haven't much to write now---Later. Love, Bud

Postmark: Fort Benning, Ga; Jan 22, 1944
Letter is on pre-printed stationery of the Second Company, First Training Regiment A.S.T.P., Fort Benning, Georgia (with logo). Jan 21, 44

Dearest Mom,

I got your letter this evening stating that you had sent a box. Swell-things keep turning up so I'll need a few things. I need seven clothes hangers if you all can spare them. I need a lock also but it's not absolutely necessary. If one of those we used at school are lying around the house you might send it but otherwise don't bother. How about a Brady Standard every once in a while. They're good to build fires with.

Mom, I'm in now--we had our final interview this evening to learn the results of our entrance (3) exams. I will be sent to a college (don't know where, & won't until I'm ready to leave) in about thirteen weeks. I will go for 12 weeks & if I make good in engineering (that's what I will study--electrical, civil, or math) I'll attend another twelve & so on for 18 months.

You mentioned pictures & I've had time but have been waiting until my hair grows out. We had our company & platoon pictures taken (yesterday) but will probably be a week or so until I hear from them.

We haven't been doing so awfully much lately. This evening I was on a detail to build steps for our Rec hall & after I got through I helped the guys G.I. the hut. By "G.I." I mean scrubbing the floor with soap & water on hands and knees--we really got the place clean. Otherwise we've been drilling, learning fundamentals, & running obstacle course (it's real tough), etc.

I got a letter from Tommy the other day & from Bob--surely was glad to hear from them. I wrote "Alvie"--ask Betty to ask him to write a guy.

Love, Bud

I do not understand the need for clothes hangers. We were limited in our wardrobe and I remember we each had a footlocker in which to put our belongings. True, we probably hung our khakis on hangers, but their quantity was limited. When we moved we merely placed all of our belongings in a barracks bag.

I am embarrassed after reading these letters as it seemed each letter home was to request either a clothes hanger, to cash a check or some other personal item.

Postmark Fort Benning, GA; Jan 20, 1944. Letter of two pages on A.S.T.P. stationery. A.S.N. 38559376; Jan 19-44. Wed night

Dearest Mater,

I got your letter with M.O. in it & one written in pencil (clippings also-thanks). I don't know whether or not I can cash it here but will see tomorrow.

We haven't done anything as yet toward starting our 13 weeks of basic except a few preliminaries, etc. I've been taking tests yesterday & today to determine whether or not I'll be sent to college when I leave here. I rather think I passed but I'm not sure & won't know until Friday.

I need an electrical plug with light socket & plug combined that you can screw in ordinary light socket. I need a mirror too if you can find a small one--at least 4" X 4". The light socket should look like this. (*A very clear drawing of the double-outlet socket was shown)*

I could get these in town if I get a pass but might not get a pass for quite a while. The mirror isn't absolutely necessary.

I hate to ask you all to trouble to pack all of these things & pay postage but I'll look forward to them an awfully lot. If any of these are too much trouble-don't bother.

I was really glad to hear from you all--it was the first mail that I had gotten since I left Camp Roberts-gets lonesome down here in the Piney woods!

How do you like this stationery? Just got it today--also took out War Bond allotment ($6.25 month)--you should receive bond in 3 months (approx.). Did you ever get an insurance policy on me? I sent you the application, if I remember right.

Got letters from Homer, Bob, and Itchie (*Itchie was Woodrow, Lindsey, a first cousin)* too today. Hot Dog! Maryellen, you write me! Jean, Bet, also---
Write, Bud

Follows is a letter to my little sister, Mary Ellen, who was fourteen years old at the time.

Postmark Jan 24, 1944; 10 AM. Letter dated Jan 22-44. (via Air Mail) Return address: Second Company, Fifth Training Regiment A.S.T.P., Fort Benning, Georgia

Dearest Maryellen,

Here it is Saturday evening — at last. We don't have anything to do tomorrow at all (unless you happened to be on K.P.) — we can sleep until we get hungry enough to get up. O, Joy!

How is everything going — Mater tells me that you're quite a social bug lately — parties, etc. Congratulations. How about that evening dress that you are going to have?

How about writing a letter to your big brother? Here I've been gone a month and a half and haven't heard from you. Incidentally, I haven't got a letter directly from home since I've been here — they all came by Camp Roberts.

There's not much to write but the chow's better & wish I could see you all.

Love, Bud

Postmark Fort Benning, Ga; Jan 24, 1944.
Jan 23-44-Sunday-4:30 PM

Dear Mom,

I slept until about 10 AM before I finally decided that I had reached a kinetic state. Most of the guys ran a fever (including myself) last night. We got two shots yesterday afternoon (tetanus & typhoid). That was my third typhoid & my first tetanus. My arm was a little sore after my first two typhoid but that was all. We all feel much better but I'm still sore.

We start our basic in the morning by falling out with full field packs--more fun!

I'm sending you an article from our newspaper, "The Pine-Bur," which we get free every Sunday. Cute huh?

I washed out my fatigues uniform yesterday afternoon. It was really dirty. Our rifles were packed in a heavy lube known as cosmoline & I got it all over me naturally. I tried to clean up my field jacket this morning but was a little hard to do.

It's really warm this evening. I had on my long-handles with wool uniform--was I cooked. We all went over to the O.C.S. (officer candidate school) post exchange looking for some herringbone twill coveralls to substitute for fatigues but couldn't find any. We can get some tomorrow if we have time.

This is the 23rd. I don't guess I'll get paid the 31st after all. Will probably get a large sum the last of February instead--so may have to send you another check soon.

In spite of the comparatively rough life we have here there's a swell spirit among us. As I told you our living conditions could be better. We gripe & beef a lot--that's how we spend our spare time. The chow's getting a lot better: the C.O. got on the mess Sgt. about it. I went to the show last night. The operators show a short reel warning us against smoking in the theater & a march is played during this reel. We all whistle the march with the music & clap when we finish.

I hope we can keep that spirit after a 15 mile hike with pack and rifle. We have so far. Our hikes (no pack & rifle yet) when on the way back we get "rest, march" someone will start singing--it's swell--makes you forget how tired you are.

The other night over here at the Recreation hall a corporal got a bunch of us together to see what we could do to amuse ourselves in what little spare time that we'll have. Musicians, singers, actors, basketball, baseball, etc, etc. I talked to him about photography but it would take a lot of red tape. I might do it though--probably won't. It'd be fun to set up a makeshift darkroom & take photos of the guys to finance it. I may have to send my cameras back---I'll see. Keep writing.

Love, Bud

P.S. I haven't got that package as yet but it's on the way I guess.

Reading this letter which mentions cosmoline reminded me of the difficult time we had removing the stuff from our rifles. It took hours to remove the grease which was like axle grease, only more tenacious. I questioned my spelling of the word "cosmoline" and looked it up in my Webster's college dictionary to find it was not listed. Of course, the spell check on my Mac was of no help. I also pulled a blank in using my small hand-held Franklin "Spelling Ace." I finally called a friend, Bill Womack, of

Midland, who had been in the 36th Division. I felt he would be familiar with the word. He was, and he found the word in a much larger dictionary. I don't recall ever seeing that word printed in anything since 1945, but I feel the Army and other branches of the service still use the stuff.

During our basic training we were shown numerous training movies, many of which the subject matter being about venereal disease, which was news to just about all of us. Sex was generally a taboo subject back in the late 30s and early 40s for a teenager as we did not have television, "R" rated movies and magazines to educate us on the finer points of such activity. Many of us were very naive about sex with our knowledge of the mysteries of the opposite sex being obtained from checking the women's lingerie section of the Sears and Roebuck catalog.

An unreliable source for information about the hard-to-find information about the feminine body was to be found by listening to my more worldly peers — peers who were perhaps two years older than I. At the time a sixteen or seventeen year old's sources were limited without asking your Dad for this information, a course of action which I evaded. You just did not get much sex education from listening to Fibber McGee and Molly and The Lux Radio Theater on the radio or watching Saturday afternoon western movies starring Tom Mix and Buck Jones who were more interested in their horses than their good looking co-stars. I was more interested in girls than I was in horses, the horse and pony phase of my yearnings passing a few years before.

The other types of movies starring Clark Gable and Carol Lombard were entertaining, but as soon as their love life in the movie got interesting the screen faded to black leaving everything that subsequently happened to our young imaginations, which were limited in scope.

One of the movies concerning venereal disease which we sat through stayed with me because it starred a very pretty young girl, portraying the girl next door. She certainly looked the part, being much like June Allison except she was a brunette. In the movie this pretty young lady went off in the bushes with this GI and he, a few days later, ended up with a terrible social disease.

Postmark Fort Benning GA; Jan 31, 1944; 9AM. (On A.S.T.P. stationery) Jan 29-44

Dear Pater,

I was glad to hear from you. Mom writes mostly--thanks for the narration.

I don't know how much the army has changed since you were a participant but I rather like it. As you know I'll have thirteen weeks of basic here then am supposed to go to college (there's a rumor that the A.S.T.P. may be disbanded). The regular infantry basic is seventeen weeks--that's what I would have gotten if I'd stayed at Camp Roberts in heavy weapons. The training here is rather mild in some respects.

We won't get quite as much hiking, however we've been on two of about four miles with light combat packs & M1 rifles last week. One of these was a practice bivouac (Friday AM) we went out to a wooded section, disbursed, marked out two slit trenches on the ground (they were strictly imaginary as we didn't have time to actually dig them) & pitched tents.

We had a couple of simulated air & artillery attacks during this time & were forced to "take cover" in the imaginary foxholes. Later on our actual bivouac will be 20 mile hike & take two weeks out of camp. They break us into it gradually.

There are lots of pine trees around but squirrels don't seem to live in pine trees. It's awfully pretty around here--I haven't been out of Ft. Benning as yet (we actually take our 20 mile bivouac within it's boundaries) but it won't compare to good old Texas.

I hear you've had some pretty good fishing lately--save a few of those 5 lb. ones for me about the last of July.

I got the package of Hershey bars (I'll bet that they were hard to find!) & fruit cake, candy, & date roll--Thanks!! Due to circumstances beyond my control, I "managed" to get rid of it all. There are 20 guys in the hut--they're swell. All are about the same age (18 or 20). I'm over at the rec hall now with Maynard-

-going to the show in a few minutes, "Ali Baba & Forty Thieves" -- got to run now. Write me again---I miss you. Love, your son, Bud

The food at Ft. Benning left a lot to be desired. It was served "family" style with the large bowls of food being placed at the head of the table by the table waiters. It didn't take us long to learn the favored seating was at the head of the table, not the foot, as the bowls would be empty before they reached the foot. I remember one meal we were served turnip greens and we had to pick out the grasshoppers from the greens.

After the evening chow we would immediately make haste to the PX, which was located at the end of the street, to see if any candy bars were available. The PX in our area at Ft. Benning was the worst one in the whole Army, Air Corps and Marines, I think.

Postmark: Fort Benning, GA, Feb 3, 1944. Letter not dated.

Dear "Littlest Sis," *(Mary Ellen)*

I couldn't figure out whose hand writing that was & didn't hardly realize whom your letter was from until I had seen the last page. You have really grown up. I hardly can realize that. Cute picture on the last page!

I'm rather tired tonight — headache also. I'm propped up in my bunk. We went on a six-mile tactical march this afternoon. You know it's funny that you can leave this place in any direction & you always travel uphill — you'd naturally think that you would go downhill coming back, but no! You come back uphill too — tiring, I think.

How's that red — or did you say "red" evening gown coming on? Wish I could see you in it. Don't get to see any body but G.I.s here — a WAAC every once in a while. You'll have to get in the WAACs when you get out of school.

I got the two boxes with sweat shirts, camera & attachments, handkerchiefs, etc. Oh, got the red flannels — tell Tommy that I'm the rage of the 2nd Co. with them. I went down to the latrine with them on and picked up a little pocket money charging the guys 10¢ a head to look.

Love & write,

Bud

Actually these were not really "red flannels" which I refer to. Back in high school I had dyed a standard pair of "long Johns" red for some idiotic occasion or perhaps a school play.

Postmark: Fort Benning, GA, Feb 7, 1944.

A.S.T.P. stationery. Feb 5, 1944

Dear Mom,

I got your large letter that you sent Virginia's outdated letter in--thanks a lot. I also got the $10.00 M.O. yesterday--thanks again. I've been a little busier lately & haven't had a chance to write. I also got the Brady Standards & magazines. I have plenty of magazines (haven't much time to read anyhow--if I get time to read I'll force myself to study a little) in the recreation but thanks a lot--send me a Standard frequently. I was only kidding about having something to start the fire with (of course, we use them for that). I like to read them.

The general attitude of the guys here seems to be that they are special, etc & will never see overseas duty. Some of us may not but, although not as soon as other branches of service, we will later after finishing our engineering study. There is a rumor (we call them latrine rumors--if you know what that is) going around to the effect that the program may be abandoned-I hope not- but could be!

We all stood inspection this afternoon & were in a parade out on the drill field-more fun! I walked guard last night for 2 hours. I'm getting used to the Army food I guess. I used to get sick at my stomach when I walked guard.

We're having a lot of training about everything in general. Went on a practice hike the other day. Shoulders aren't bothering me so much now so forget my request for padding. I don't need a thing now except coat hangers--I guess you sent them didn't you?

I'll try to call you next Sunday night if I can. I may try to call this Sun--Max did pay me but haven't cashed the Western Union M.O. as yet. I got $5 from Sea biscuit (*this must refer to Alex Houston who bought my Cushman motor scooter when I left for the Army)* also that he owed me on the scooter. I'm going to buy a $25 bond about Monday--we'll get paid about Wed--I hope!

Love, Bud Write

P.S. Tell Ernest that I like that service of small town P.O.(*I have no idea what this means. It must refer to the good postal employees in Brady)*

Postmark for the following letter was March 9, 1944, but the letter was written in February. Perhaps it was placed in the wrong envelope? After looking at all of the letters which had a March postmark but were written in February, I can only guess that the postal stamp was wrong at Fort Benning, i.e. set for March instead of February and no one noticed or did not know how to change the date on the machine which imprinted the postmark. This remains one of the small, unsolved mysteries of WWII.

Feb 8-44, Wed night, 8:45 PM

Dearest Mom,

I got your Brady papers that you sent-thanks! Also a letter from Jean.

I've got a full week this week. We've been on day firing range. We'll go out on the wet range in the morning to fire the carbine for record. It's cold and clear out--a little too cold for firing but the second company won't fire until in the afternoon so we won't do so bad. I have to get up about 5:30 AM to work in the pits before the rest get out--no doubt, because of my superior ability!

There's something cooking here--we don't know what yet but you can tell by the way the officers act--remarks-jokes, etc. I was down at the latrine last night--let me see, I was on the third stool & this other fellow who I was talking to was on the fifth. Says he heard that we will be moved shortly--it's definite that we'll be here for another week--after that we don't know--closer to home I hope.

'night, Bud

I'm on K.P. tomorrow night & all day Friday--guard last night--big moon and cold (wonderful).

The Army's communal barracks' toilet facility, or latrine, was the best and most reliable source of information available except directly from the First Sergeant or the Company Commander. Some of this information was amazingly accurate and it was impossible to trace the data to its source.

It would have been difficult to obtain a pass during our stay at Ft. Benning. Of course, the cadre could do so and we were all very interested where they went while on a three day pass.

Ft. Benning was located on the western edge of Georgia, near the Georgia-Alabama border, and Columbus, Georgia. Just across the border in Alabama was the town of Phenix City, which we heard was a very sinful place, having gambling, prostitutes and honkytonks galore. I suppose, given the chance, most of us might have visited this sinful city, but, alas, the opportunity did not arise.

Postmark: Feb 10, 1944; Fort Benning, GA. Feb 9-44; Wed-9:20 AM

Dear Mom,

We have a little free time this morning--something unusual! We went on a night problem last night & were back by 12, but have until 10:30 to ourselves. I'll have to take a couple of shots before then, I guess. They'll have someone down from the orderly room shortly looking for some of us.

I was able to sleep late this morning by skipping chow--got up & washed up--don't have time for such luxury often. I'm still learning a lot--gets more serious--no picnic. No doubt, I'll be a hard man-ha!

Also still have a little fun. One of the guys found a "KP" sign & hung it on the foot of one of the other guy's bed. He naturally thought that he was going on K.P.; consequently, he went down to the kitchen the next morning & made a fool of himself. He deserved it as he is one of the few "sad-sacks" of the company.

Don't send that developer & hypo (*dark room processing chemicals*) that I asked for--I won't have time I can see--might get in trouble , too. I'd like that popcorn though--would hit the spot some Sat. night.

It rained last night after we got in & showered in on me from open shutter--didn't last long so I let it rain in. I feel swell this morning. Peppy, etc--Been taking my "Carter's Little Liver Pills" regularly, you know.

I'll send those films if I ever make it over to the P.O. We've been having to fall out so quickly at lunch time that I haven't had a chance to get over.

Our laundry service is really wonderful--we get it back once a week. You never know what you're going to get back. Different sizes, colors, articles &

everything. I haven't gotten any feminine articles back yet--looking forward to the time.

Got to run-- Love, "G.I." Bud (*Afterthought was written on the back outside of the envelope along the flap line, "Wish I had some clothes hangers")*

Post mark on the following letter's envelope was Mar 14, 1944, but the letter is dated Feb 12-44.

Feb 12-44, 7:00 PM, Sunday

Dear Mom,

I'm in what is known as a tent city (no doubt Dad knows what it is)--six men to each. This is out on the range where we'll fire for record. We have all of the modern conveniences--running water (cold)(when it rains); heated tents (by candles); deluxe latrines (12 holes); modern air conditioning (through sides of tent); indirect lighting (through flaps & by candles), etc, etc.

Oh-but you should have seen me last night! We marched about eleven or twelve miles in a combination downpour & drizzle; then pitched 4-man tents on the cold, cold (& wet)--got up at about four this morning & continued through another eight miles of mud to our "homes." It wasn't so bad--we all got up this morning & three of us would wring the fourth out until we were only damp.

We fired the carbine the other day--I made 172 out of possible 200. 175 was "Expert"--160 for "Sharpshooter." I'll see what I can do with the M1.

We got some more pictures of a platoon (3rd) group this time (about 70 men)--I'll send you one when I get them.

I shaved in a helmet of cold water this afternoon.

We'll be here a week & probably won't get a chance to take a bath until I get back. I've just discovered an ingenious method of setting up a 2-candle power (literally speaking) light by my bed (yes a G.I. bed with springs)--I inverted my canteen up-tied it to a support & put two candles on the bottom--wonderful!

We have a seventh occupant in the tent--that I failed to mention. We've been chasing him all evening trying to catch him--it's a little mouse--evasive, too!

I got a letter from Ola day before yesterday--she sent me Jack's (*this must refer to Jack Best*) address--5th company. I can assume that Jack is in the A.S.T.P. if he hasn't shipped out--but I'll be dern if I can guess, not being psychic, which Regt or Bn he's in. Smart girl-your sister.

Love, Bud

Postmark on letter was Fort Benning, GA, March 15, 1944, 10 AM. Date on letter was Feb 13-44, Monday 8:30 PM, Tent City

Dear Mom,

My nightly communique---

I didn't fire today but worked all day in the "pits" on targets (after the war I'll build myself a range on G.I. principal)--I really worked too. It was cold enough for overcoats when we went out this morning but I had to take my long handles off right after lunch (the sun was actually out). I got all dusty & tired--came back to the "city" about 5:30 PM & found that some kind soul had lifted the flaps of all of the tents cooling them off--nice. I took a good cold bath & facial (shampoo too) in a helmet full of water & feel very invigorated.

The mobile PX truck rolled up & I actually fought my way to it (luckily I had my bayonet with me) & went on a spending spree indulging in a soda pop & four bits of other oddities seldom seen hereabouts.

I got your letter today giving my bank statement. Thanks! --& I guess I will send my letter "free."

Yes, I got a letter from Ola thanking me for a company picture that I sent her. She said that she was going down to Uncle Baker's soon & would stop by Brady. Uncle Baker keeps getting worse doesn't he. I wish that I could see him again.

Corporal (Murphy SNAFU) Millman & his "Hungry Five" were entertaining the Regt. during chow until got too dark. They are our Bn. band--pretty good--played Retreat, too. Corp. Millman usually plays the part of the humorous dumb & hopeless G.I. in our demonstrations during training so we call him "Murphy."

Love, Bud

P.S. I think our "seventh occupant" left for tent 39--must be the odor.

Of all of the military acronyms, the Army's "SNAFU", is probably the best known, both in the Army and civilian life. The polite unraveling of its meaning would be, "Situation Normal, All Fouled Up."

Postmark: Fort Benning, GA, Feb 14, 1944, 2 PM. Feb 13-44 Sunday.

Dearest Mom,

I got your box of cookies, clothes hangers & candy--we (20 of us--Hut #61) enjoyed every crumb--thanks. No, seriously I put away the box of Toll

House cookies for myself--thanks. For the towels & safety pins too--I don't guess I'll need any padding after all--thank heavens--they work us into all of this rather gradually so that I hardly notice my rifle & pack now. *(All of us experienced sore shoulders from firing the M1 rifle. Our shoulders would be bruised..black & blue.)*

Did Harry send you a check--if you haven't already deposited it, send it back to him. I don't want him to pay me for that motor. If you have already deposited it, tell me so I can send him a M.O. How do you like this snappy stationery he sent me? Swell of him wasn't it?

We got paid Friday--I got $43 & a few cents--I bought a $37.50 bond with what Maxine sent me ($13.95) & have difference in pocket & will get paid again last of Feb. I spent a little on three company pictures ($1 each) & stationery.

The company pictures were in black & white, showed the entire company and were 30 inches long by 8 inches high. The picture displayed 257 officers and men. The photography work was by Maurice Photo Service, Columbus, GA. Dial 9336, Box 1413. All are dressed in "wools." The letter continues...

I'm sending you a company picture (Ola & Virginia, too) (*Ola refers to my Aunt Ola, Virginia was a girl friend)* It's not very good of me but pin it up so that it won't ruin the pleasant home like surroundings of 1103 S. China.

Being in the Army gives you a chance to study those about you, Mom. I'm glad I'm like I am--wish I was more like some others though. Paul Linder sleeps just above me (I'll mark members of hut on picture) is really swell--he's from Iowa. Rather quiet & doesn't have any outward evident grand ideas about himself as do a bunch of us.

It's been awfully cold here the last couple of days. I was finally issued two pair of long handles--came in handy. The sand was wet Friday & Sat morning was very solid--frozen. Clear as a whistle though.

Tell M.E.(Mary Ellen) that I really appreciated the picture of Sinatra (irony) & those pictures were really swell--hit the nail right on the head!

Tell Betty that one of V. was pretty good photography--can't say much for likeness of Shorty though. That must have been quite a snow.

Love, Bud

P.S. Thanks for the Valentine, Mom--you're about the only Valentine I need. Bud

Ola sent me a sewing kit that really comes in handy!

Postmark Fort Benning, GA, Feb 16, 1944, 3 PM

Dearest Mom,

Maybe so I should go over to the hut & go to bed. It gets pretty comfortable in that G.I. bunk about 6:30 AM.

It's been sloppy all day--tends to dampen (take me literally there) your spirits--but feel great. I really got wet this evening. My shoe soles are worn through & my feet got wet (too). Were issued two pair of shoes but I have one pair sent in to be half soled--pretty good wearing out two pair in a month!

I got the magazines & Brady Standard this

evening-thanks. I haven't sent the company pictures as yet--haven't had time, but will do so as soon as I can.

We actually saw some girls today. Five girls came to visit our company--ate in the mess hall with us--one at our table. We had to act like gentlemen--we couldn't even cuss the table waiters out--bad! Tell Jean that one did have a southern accent..Gertrude!

This reference to "Gertrude" requires some explanation. Back at Cobb's Drug Store in Brady, there were several of us working. Most of the time we had three behind the counter, sometimes four. Usually a couple of us were males, all teenagers and acutely conscious of any young, attractive female who came to the soda fountain. One of us would call out, "Gertrude in three," or "Agnes in two," or perhaps another girls name, with the "three" or "two" being the designated site of their seating; i.e. the booth number. The name which we called out would tell the other of our rating of the looks of the young female, Gertrude not being the highest rate, a "ten." I forget the name we assigned to a real knockout, but as far as I know the customers thought it was some type of order we called. It was a adolescent and impolite type of activity, but we were young and thought we were very smart. Which we weren't. The letter continues...

I would have called yesterday but didn't have a

chance when line was clear--we have one telephone per Bn (*battalion*)--you can imagine what it's like trying to get a call through--egad!

A few of the guys have the flu out of the hut--Paul Linden (grouped alphabetically) stayed in the hut today--he's a swell guy--wish you could meet him.

What's this about Bob Best being here. I don't think that I could possibly remember him. What connection did we have? What is he in Armored, Inf., or Paratroopers (Surely hasn't the misfortune to be in the A.S.T.P.)

Must run. Love, Bud

Postmark Fort Benning, GA, Feb 21, 1944, 4:30 PM. Sat, 6:30 PM, Feb 19, 1944

Dear Mom,

It's still wet here--they issued life belts yesterday for use in the low places. It's so wet that I have web feet.

Mater, it looks like your son is back in the regular infantry. This rumor is rather official this time--most of the program is folding up. I don't know how it'll affect me (us still in basic) as yet--will probably get four more weeks of basic whether here or somewhere else. I don't know much of anything about it yet--will know Monday.

Tonight we of Hut 61 enjoy the comforts of modern (comparatively so) lighting. For the last three days we have risen & went to bed; rolled our packs; made our bunks; & tried (ahem) to write letters by lights from the stove. Some one managed to talk the supply sergeant out of a couple of Dad's lanterns so we had romantic subdued light last night. Wonderful! We had to clean our rifles by two of these for inspection today. I worked with vigor & enthusiasm (as usual) on my rifle & Lt. Allen didn't even look at it--Paul Linder & I both--he gave a careful inspection of all other 18. The only plausible theory that I can offer is that he is aware of our ability & knowing that it was useless to try to find anything wrong with them didn't bother to look (ahem!). & besides we bunk over in a dark corner where he can't see his hand in front of his face.

We've been awfully busy--no hikes, too. I haven't had a chance to write to anyone; consequently, I haven't had much fan mail pouring in--as usual. I got a letter at noon from you--no couldn't use the electric popper--that's one thing that I couldn't roll up in my comfort or put behind a picture to hide from inspecting officer.

If I ever get into the main post I'll try to get myself a waterproof & luminous dial watch--so don't be surprised if I send one home (my Elgin).

'night. Love, Bud

P.S. Pardon my rambling style of letters--hope they don't appear boring to you--must have got it from the Shannon side of the family, no?

Postmark Fort Benning, GA, Mar 7, 1944, 4:30 PM (Has a 6¢ airmail stamp...stamps on most of the envelopes have been removed) March 6, 1944, 9:45

This envelope had a 6¢ air mail stamp affixed. Earlier envelopes had 8¢ air mail stamps. Could it be possible the U.S.P.O. went down on their air mail rates?

Dearest Mom,

Just a short note tonight--just got a letter from

Jack. He's back in the U.S. at Goldthwaite. He's going back to work at Kelly Field but is 1A--will probably be drafted. Gee I'm happy to know that he's back.

I got the cookies at noon--we liked them an awfully lot (I still have about half of them for myself)-thanks a lot.

Forgive the short letter--everthing's fine--busy as heck. I've got to inflate my water wings & go to the latrine.

'night Love ya, Bud

At Ft. Benning the latrine, containing the commodes, wash basins and showers, was in a separate building, unlike the better facilities in most other Army posts.

One person who was an ASTPer said the huts were first used to house Italian POWs, but the Red Cross or another authority raised so much heck about their being inadequate they moved the Italians to regular Army barracks. Evidently the tar paper huts were deemed satisfactory for the ASTPers.

Working the pits at the rifle range consisted of standing in a trench below the targets and moving a marker, a large red disc mounted on a long pole, over the target indicating the location of the bullet hole after each round was fired from that station. If the target was missed completely we waved a red flag which was called "Maggie's Drawers." One G.I.

wrote of his rifle range experience as he, being a good shot, would shoot the red disc on the adjoining target when it was put up to spot the result of the fellow next to him. This crossed my mind, but I declined. Actually it would have been good practice at a moving target as it would require good coordination.

Postmark on envelope is Mar 17, 1944, 9AM, Fort Benning, GA. Letter is dated Feb 15-44, 8:00 PM, Wed. Unlike most of the others, this one is written in pencil.

Dear Pater,

Well, Pater, I didn't do as good as an old Texas squirrel hunter should do. This was mainly because they wouldn't let me shoot from the hip. No, I shot 178 out of a possible 210. I am known as a sharpshooter--180 was expert (my goal)--165 was minimum for sharpshooter so you can see that I'm slightly sick because if I had have only took a little more time on two of those 4's I would have something to be proud of.

It's been another swell day--we were all hot & dusty (& tired) when we came in at 5 after being out since 7:30. Five of us out of the tent went down to a creek about 600 yards from the "city" & took our first bath in several days. It is really a nice creek, about 40 feet across & 4 feet deep in deepest part where we were, a good sandy & gravel bottom & cold--ice cold. It really revived me--I could shoot 209 now. One fine young man did shoot 200 in our platoon.

I got a swell four page letter from Jean & my returned check. Thank her for me & tell her that that was a very well composed letter. I'll write her as soon as I can. I have to get my rifle cleaned. They're hard to clean after firing. Cpl. Millman & his "Hungry Five" are giving out down the company street (?).

Love, Bud

P.S. We really get wonderful chow here--much better than back at camp. With the same cooks, too--remarkable! We go out to fire the machine (light) & 60mm mortar--more fun.

I felt sorry for some of the men in our company as they had never handled a rifle before getting in the army. I was very well trained in the use of pistols and rifles, being tutored by my father who was an avid hunter and fisherman, when he had the time after selling Singer Sewing Machines, repairing the same and teaching little ladies how to adjust and use their machines. Many were the mornings on weekends when Dad and I were in position under a large pecan tree on Lost Creek before daylight to wait for the squirrels to emerge.

As I am left-handed and shoot a rifle left-handed, it was somewhat awkward to handle any rifle, it being an M1 Army rifle or a Remington hunting rifle, as they are all designed for a right-handed person. Actually the only two problems were that it ejected the spent 30 caliber case across your face and you could not force a new clip into the magazine as fast as a right-handed person

Postmark is Mar 21, 1944, Fort Benning, GA,

4PM. Letter is dated Feb 19-44, Sun evening 6:30 PM. The letter is directed to sister, Dorothy Jean.

Dear Sis,

I got your letter (well composed) with the check in it. I will take it back but will pay for my calls in the future. Thanks for the compliments, gal.

We're back at camp now--came in last night--I didn't have my water wings along so I almost drowned. No kidding every time we take a hike we have three inches of rain. I think the C.O. waits for the Army meteorologist to predict a good rain before he schedules a hike. We left at 7:30 PM (Sat) & got in about one this morning. We all have raincoats but I'd rather get soaking wet than have to hike in the raincoat. It started off in a drizzle (not enough to bother with raincoats) & by the time that it really started raining we were soaked to a point where we didn't care. Incidentally, it"s raining outside now--egad!

I got the book while I was out at the "city" (no, I didn't carry it back in the rain--we were allowed a barracks bag of clothes & personal belongings--mostly food).

I've read almost half of it this evening & it's darn good, don't you think?

We all fired the 60mm mortar the other day — fun! Also I managed to qualify on the light machine gun — 193 out of 256 — 180 was qualifying — 218 was expert.

Well, Sis, we've finally found out what is going to happen to us. We're moving north to S. Carolina early this week. We're supposed to use secrecy in such matters and eliminate place & time. I'll be in the Inf. unless my papers should call for something else.

I'm sure that they don't however as only about eight men will be left here. We'll all be together--that's nice.

I'll be in a P.O.R. *(pool of replacements)* ready to go over whenever they should need a good G.I. on some South Pacific island or somewhere.

Love, Bud

Gee — A dry bed & comparatively dry hut tonight — Shangrila!

(*Note on the back of the envelope, along the sealed flap:* Stop all but 1st class mail)

The A.S.T.P. program was scrapped by Washington and I, along with untold numbers of eighteen-year olds, were moved from their basic training sites and colleges to regular army outfits. Most of us at Ft. Benning went to the 100th Infantry Division which was at Ft. Bragg, North Carolina.

CHAPTER FOUR

FORT BRAGG, NORTH CAROLINA

Postmark: Fort Bragg, N.C., Mar 27, 1944, 4:30 PM. Letter is dated March 25, 44, Sunday, 11:00 AM:" 397 Inf. Regt., Co F, A.P.O. 447, Ft. Bragg, N.C.

Dear Mom,

We're finally settled a little--getting everything straightened out, etc. It's a little different here--hard to get used to. We actually have good barracks, chow, P.X., & theater. We were moved as a bunch but we're split up over three regiments. There are a few guys from the former second company in Company F but more from the hut. Paul Linder & a few others are in Co. L. I'm in a rifle company--on a B.A.R. (*Browning Automatic Rifle)* team. The trip up from Benning was wonderful. We spent twenty-four hours in a day coach. I can't imagine where the "Georgia Central RR" got that coach unless it was from Republic or Universal pictures (they had been using it in old westerns).

I mailed a camera back just before I left--store it away somewhere. Also, I sent a platoon picture--tack it up on a convenient wall somewhere & don't let it bother you too much. Tell Jean to look at Corp. Fuientas--he's really a swell guy--known throughout the regt. as being most human corp. present. Corp. Webb is in charge of our hut (61) - he's swell also. Lt Allen was tops--wish you could meet them all.

We haven't done much as yet--I got up early this morning & washed out a bunch of clothes. It's warm out--real nice.

I finished that book on the train. I really enjoyed it. I'll send it back as soon as I find the P.O. around here.

In a week or so if you have any extra clothes

hangers I could use about four, but can get along without them.

Chow time, must close. Love, Bud

Postmark March 28, 1944, Fort Bragg, N.C.. Letter dated March 27, 44. 397 Inf. Regt., A.P.O. 447, Co. F, Ft. Bragg, N.C.

Dear Mom, Just a short note; the main cause of which being my financial status. Haven't really any news to give you & no letters from you to answer so wouldn't write if I wasn't broke. Am enclosing a check for $10.00--send it in cash registering or insuring it. I don't even have my dog tags at present so it's pretty hard to identify myself (naturally I'll achieve regimental fame shortly--but it'll take a few days for the rest of the regt. to realize that they have a genius in their midst!)

As I say we haven't done anything as yet much. We're going to take the same old training over for about three or four weeks for the benefit of a few fellows who hadn't received as much basic back at Benning as we had--it's awfully monotonous (sp?)

Write. Love you, Bud

I have no idea why I did not have my dog-tags, as I would have thought they would have been issued back at the Fort Sam Houston Reception Center in San Antonio when I went in the Army.

The dog-tags listed your name, Army serial number, your blood type and religious preference. They hung on a chain around your neck at all times, even while showering. Should you be killed in action, the dog tags were a positive form of identification. Should you be wounded, the blood type was apparent, thus saving time should you require a transfusion. I would think the reason the religious preference was shown on the tags would be in case last rites were spoken over you.

These are the reasons not explained to us, but were apparent after giving the matter some thought.

Postmark Fort Bragg, N.C., March 29, 1944, 12 M. Letter dated March 28, 44. Tues, 6:30 PM.

Dear Pater,

I got your letter this evening just before chow. I was awfully glad to hear from you -- first mail I've gotten since I left Benning.

That's very interesting about your army shooting-- I've probably heard you tell a lot of your experiences but didn't register as well as they do now. Have a lot to tell you when I get home--maybe in a couple of months. It's easier to get furloughs & passes in a regular outfit.

I'm in the 100th Division, 397 Regt. The first man to receive the new "Expert Infantry Badge" is out of our outfit. He will be decorated Wed (tomorrow) & we will be part of the audience. Life and Time newspapers galore are covering the occasion-- exciting.

The badge is pretty hard to qualify for--stress on physical fitness, etc. They have a grade of "Ranger" here too. It's hard to make also (my ambition).

As I told you before we're getting an extended or refresher course of basic. Some of the guys that haven't had the chance to qualify with the M1 will go on the range--we may too but probably won't fire again. (dern it!).

We new men all moved into one barracks--tried to put most of us on the bottom floor, too. There are about 35 beds (no double-deckers, however) on the bottom floor. We have guys from all over--even Texas. One boy is from McAllen (Kayser).

Speaking of fishing--you should have seen some of the little streams in Georgia. They were all over the place--not very big or deep, but cold & looked like good trout streams.

Write. Love, Bud

The Expert Infantryman Badge was a pretty badge and exclusive to the Army infantry. I coveted this badge when they were first announced and shown. Later I did earn the badge. I also had a good conduct metal, which was much easier to earn than the Expert Infantryman badge. If you stayed out of trouble, you automatically earned a Good Conduct Metal, a metal which was easy for me to earn, difficult for some others.

Postmark, Fort Bragg, N.C., April 4, 1944, 10 AM. Letter dated Apr 3, 1944, 397 Inf. Regt. #38 559 376, Co. F APO447, Ft. Bragg, N.C., 8:30 PM

Dearest Mom,

I got a letter from you late this afternoon--awfully

glad to hear from you--be happier when I get the cash for the check--along with a good long rambling letter, so typical of you (a compliment whether you know it or not).

I feel great this evening & reckless also. I actually had 29¢ in my pocket--felt so exuberant & reckless (etc) that I took invigorating shower, shave (etc) & dashed down to the PX & expended 15¢ of my precious 29 on a pt. of vanilla--was wonderful.

I'm not on the BAR any more--was moved to the trainees then back again--don't know what I'll be now--probably a flank guard on the rifle team. The BAR is the Browning Auto. Rifle (rather like the British "Sten Gun") - a little heavier (about twice as) than our Grands (M1) & can really put out the fire power. Takes 3 men on a BAR team. Dad probably knows about it--was used in the last war, I believe, as is now except for a few minor improvements.

Tell Dad to save a few of those .22 shells--won't need many. I'm strictly a one shot man.

The chow is still wonderful & plenty of it--if we don't start more hard work here in a few days or so, I'll get fat.

I've actually found someone who can fix Mexican style beans better than you--if you'll forgive me for saying so. The only thing that we're short on is milk & sugar.

Bring on the cookies (& $10) by all means. Bud

Postmark Fort Bragg, N.C., April 9, 1944, 11:30 AM. Letter dated Apr 8-44, 9 PM, Sat. night.

Dear Squirrel Hunter (*this refers to Dad)*,

Thanks for the $10--was awfully glad to get--incidentally though of minor importance compared to the $10, was glad to hear from you also--now don't let it go to your head!

Finally started to work a little. We went out on a daylight problem last week. One platoon on the defensive and & other on offensive. I was on the offensive & was leading scout for our squad which was lots of fun--it's just like squirrel hunting only different--more work. I don't believe I was hit only 8 or 10 times. Naturally we were using blanks.

Yes, that was the tech. Sgt. that won the medal--a lot of the older men are winning them--will get myself one someday. Right now I'm rather a flop. Also got a bunch of Brady papers yesterday--thanks!

I got a letter from Mom with V-Mail from Kendall (*Kendall was first cousin...Ola's son)*--will write him shortly.

Tell Mom that that cake hasn't arrived as yet but I can visualize it a light billowy fluffy mass of vitamins packed egg white blended with perfection cooked sugar syrup combined with ??, etc. to create a beautiful delicious cake that will probably be in a shape to defy all geometric designs when it reaches me--we'll see--looking forward to it very much! She mentioned pop corn--don't send any. I can't pop it here. I still have a little of the other left.

I went down to the dental clinic & spent all of the morning getting my tooth back in--looks better than it did--turned my old tooth in for salvage!

Must go to barracks & get to bed. Am a table waiter (form of K.P.) tomorrow--can't even go to church.

Your offspring, Bud

While in high school in Brady, I developed an abscess in a tooth...a front tooth. At the time a dentist didn't know anything except to yank the tooth out, which he did and then ordered a single false tooth. One day while we were practicing hand-to-hand fighting, someone knocked out the false tooth. I then was sent to the army dentist, where he repaired the damage and installed a GI model tooth.

Postmark Fort Bragg, N.C., Apr 12, 1944, 12:30 PM. Letter dated Apr 11-44, 4:40 PM, Tues.

Dearest Mom,

We just got in off of the range--took a shower & took some clothes down to the cleaners. I've got a little time before we fall out for "retreat."

It's finally warmed up to a point where it's uncomfortable at times. I spent all day yesterday & most of today out on the range as a coach for the guys who hadn't fired & were doing so. I fired a few rounds off the record just to have something to do every now & then--got a little sunburned on my face.

I like it here more & more--you are more your own boss & don't have a bunch of noncoms who have to watch you.

We got paid yesterday so I'm a little ahead--will keep that $10 & won't replace it as yet--will get paid again the 1st. I'm going to look around to see if I can get me a fair waterproof watch also a good pair of sunglasses. I lost my sunglasses on the infiltration course (mental cond. course) at Benning & wasn't able to get them back. Ask Jean to keep her eyes open for a $10 (or less) pair like I have there at home--they're pretty hard to find. I can buy a regular service watch in the main P.X. here I think cheap.

I haven't got the cake as yet but haven't had mail call today.

Also went down to P.X. this afternoon & got a couple of bottles of milk--don't have milk any too often. You should see some of the cute girls that work in some of the P.X.s--the environment around here is wonderful. I'll go to the show tonight no doubt.

Love, Bud

P.S. just had 1/2 of our mail call--got a letter from Betty. Write! Bud

Postmark Fort Bragg, N.C., Apr 17, 1944, 4:30 PM. Letter dated Apr 16-44, Sun Afternoon, 5:45 PM

Dear Mom,

Mon, 8:00 AM

Just got the letter started yesterday evening when McKee came dashing up & wanted to do something, so we went over to the main post & went to the show. The main post is really a swell place compared to this "outpost." The officers' homes remind me of some homes in Angelo--wide streets--beautiful homes (all alike) & good lawns, etc.

I guess I have the morning off--the life of a goldbrick, ah yes. The company went out on a problem a little bit ago & won't be back until late this afternoon. We have to be over at Regt. HQ at 1:30 PM--sooo I loaf (unless the 1st Sgt. finds me) this A.M.

When summer or spring hits N.C. it goes in for it 100%--it's been awfully warm the last week--still rains though. This is the 17th--we go into our khakis the first of May--will be a change. I'll try to get my picture made before we switch. They have a photo service over at the main post in P.X.--can't say much for the quality in proportion to the price, but they'll do.

I guess Tommy is gone by now, yes? I haven't heard from him--like to see him. Homer *(Homer Pearsall from Alice)* is still in Washington as far as I know. I haven't heard from Harold (*this would be Harold Davis from Alice, Texas)* -- do you have his overseas address? I've got to write Kendall soon as I get more stamps for air mail. Love, Bud

Postmark Fort Bragg, N.C., Apr 18, 1944, 4:30 PM. Letter dated Apr 18-44, 10:45 AM, Tues. Morning.

Dearest Mom,

We've got the morning off again as the company went out & will be gone all day. Haven't a thing to do--got my laundry back & sorted it out, etc. The Sarge. found Seamons (the other Pvt. going to scout school) & I yesterday morning so we went on table-waiters for a couple of hours. The "school" is going to be interesting--lot of work later on. There are three of us from the company going--Seamons, a buck Sarge., & I.

I got your letter with Ola's & the play announcement in it--thanks!

Watch for the 100th Div. in newspapers--Life, etc. We had a demonstration for some brass the other day. I wasn't in it--wish I could have been--but we could hear the artillery from the barracks. It was strictly a fire-power demonstration--was good.

Mike Marcos (Penn.) (*Mike Marcos was from*

Burgettestown, PA) is in the "school" with me--he was back at Benning in our hut (the widely acclaimed #61). I see a lot of the old bunch in the P.X. & at the theater. All of the boys who shipped, left this morning--hated to see them go. Some are in the Field Artillery now.

Write. Love, Bud

P.S. George Locker must have read or looked at the book on the train coming up--I don't know him very well--not in either picture. I haven't heard from Jack as yet--don't know what happened to him. We'll write soon as he gets in the Army.

I still have one camera--will try to get it registered. If I can't do so I may send it back but will probably hang on to it to use when I go into town, etc. Bud

I have no memory about a requirement to register a camera, but this must have been the case. I do know it was strictly forbidden to photograph places and things such as a beach scene, military installation or bridge over a major river.

Postmark Fort Bragg, N.C., Apr 22, 1944, 12 M. Letter dated Apr 21(I think!), 10:20 PM, Fri night.

Dear Pater,

I was glad to hear from you this evening at mail call--your brief epic on squirrel hunting reminded me of some of the good old days. It used to be pretty cold about daylight with frost all over, yes?

I'm sending you a practice bazooka (sp?) shell--it's perfectly harmless--we use them for practice.

Before being fired they have a propelling charge but no explosive charge in the head. Although the practice bazooka shell (M1) is no military secret don't display it around too much. You might clean it up a little give it a light coat of oil & put it together & put it in what was formerly my (?) room. I'm sending it in four parts---nomenclature follows:

(I drew a rough drawing of the practice shell identifying the parts)

I found the thing coming in from the "transition range"--did OK on the firing this morning--shot a possible. We had 120 seconds to fire 10 rounds at six targets (silhouettes). Two at two hundred; two at three hundred; & two at five hundred. I just had to shoot six rounds.

I got a letter from Harold--in England. He says that it's fairly miserable. There's a very strong rumor this evening that we will be moved to POE (Port Of Embarkation) about middle of May--afraid that it may be true--we'll see.

Scout school still rolls along. We really haven't done too much--compass work, map reading, etc.--rather interesting.

Write soon & take care of my souvenir, Bud

A "possible" when on a rifle range means you have shot the highest score possible on a target. I was pretty good thanks to my father's tutoring in my early years.

Postmark Fort Bragg, N.C., apr 24, 1944, 2:30 PM. Letter dated Apr 23-44, Sun night, 8:45.

Dearest Mom,

I just got in from the main post--went over to see the show, etc. I slept all morning--didn't go to church as I should have!

I made my first (& probably my last) trip into the grand & thriving metropolis of Fayetteville, North Carolina. It's larger than Brady & G.I.s galore. It could be worse, I guess. Took in a show & bought some briefs & T shirts & came on back to camp after standing in a bus line for about 45 minutes or an hour.

I found a you-hold-the-camera-and-take-the-picture-while-we-take-your quarter booth & proceeded to experiment further into the depths of photography--enclosed are poor examples--look at them then burn them.

Say, North Carolina isn't so bad in spite of Fayetteville & Ft. Bragg. Pine trees (& sand) & rolling hills--the weather has been swell & it's really nice. Tell Dad that I haven't seen any squirrels but there are a lot of deer around. We saw four or five walk out of the woods into Pope Field while we were out on the range which is near there.

Write, Bud

I refer to "briefs" which would really be shorts, I suppose. The Army issued olive drab boxer type of shorts for underwear which were perfectly adequate so I really don't understand, fifty-odd years later, why I would want to buy "briefs" in Fayetteville.

Mother, being an excellent seamstress through having been working with Dad in the Singer Sewing

Machine business, made my shorts, shirts and most of the girl's clothes. Those were they days when it was customary to salvage suitable cloth material from such articles as flour sacks, which were made into clothes. A noted Texas vendor of flour, Burris Mills, sold their flour in popular sacks which were coveted by the women. They also sponsored a band of the early 30's known as The Light Crust Dough Boys, who were most helpful in getting W. Lee O'Daniels elected as Governor of Texas, as they toured with him while he was campaigning for that office.

Postmark Fort Bragg, N.C., Apr 25, 1944, 12M. Letter dated Apr 25-44, 9:00 PM, Tues.

Dearest Mom,

I made it! Hooray! We came stumbling in about 3:00 this afternoon-- seven hours--25 miles. It was easier than I expected. I made it OK, except for the last 24 miles, it was a snap. I saw a lot of country anyway. It was a clear & warm day so we were pretty hot when we got in--that shower really did a grand job of recuperation for me.

How's Snafu now--you keep telling me he's bigger? What breed of a dog would you say he was?.

We haven't heard any more about our POE--Frankly I don't think that I'll be in on it. Some of the older men may be taken for replacements but we're a long ways from being ready. The fellows that came up from Benning that had less than 8 weeks of training are under a special training program for at least another week. After next week they will probably be put in the regular company. Not much to write--more next time. I'm affected with what is known as bunk fatigue...night, Love, Bud

I found, as did most G.I.s, you could doze while marching in a column on a long march. The trick was to obtain a position in the middle of the group (not on the edge). You could actually cat nap as you marched, waking periodically to check your bearings.

Postmark: Fort Bragg, N.C., April 28, 6:30 PM. Letter dated Apr 27-44, Thurs Night. Return address, Co F, 397 Inf. Regt., APO 447, Ft. Bragg, N.C.

Dearest ME, (*This letter to Mary Ellen, little sister)*

Was quite happy to stroll nonchalantly into the barracks (home) & find tucked neatly under the pillow covering a combination letter from you and Jean. I've been on K.P. all day (quite tiring) & just got off a little while ago. Peeled potatoes most of afternoon!

How could you tell that SNAFU just grinned — maybe he was yawning or laughing — can't quite picture a grin — give me a mental picture, gal.

Now I don't want any bickering in our happy little family so have splurged & purchased you a patch also. I'm getting some regimental insignias also to put on blouse & cap, etc.

Tell Jean that I got her letter this evening after chow (I rate two letters a day!) with the pictures of Chandler's in it. I'll send them back tomorrow as I know she wants them back.

We all pulled our beds <u>again</u> today. The training men joined the company. This new arrangement gives us about 5 inches instead of six between beds.

Must get my beauty sleep, Love,

Bud

P.S. Hooray! My hair has grown out a little. In fact I actually need a haircut.

Postmark Fort Bragg, N.C., May 5, 1944, 12:30 PM. Letter dated May 4-44, 10PM.

Dear Pater,

Haven't long to write--it's getting rather late. I think I owe everybody that I've ever known a letter including you. By looks of the furlough list I guess I will be able to join you on one of those squirrel hunts--thanks for asking me.

Jean, hold up on those glasses for a while--I find that I don't make quite as much money as I used to. It's good for me--I'm not complaining (not bragging, though).

I'm still going to scout school--still interesting. I go out in the mornings with the company then go to scout school in the afternoon. This morning I went out with the company about two or three miles & was lucky enough to catch a vehicle back in.

I went over to the main post via foot through the woods the other evening about six. I had plenty of time so I employed some of the principals of jungle fighting & what I have learned at scout school & was able to see a deer (again). She happened to be a medium sized doe--about 25 yards was as close as I was able to get. I'll unlimber my camera someday I think & get some good color pictures of her or another.

Jack is in the Navy for sure--he's at Goldthwaite now waiting to be called into active duty. At least he won't have to walk much further than the length of the ship.

Write me...Love, Bud

How about letting me know my bank balance again & sending me a pocket check book. Thanks.

In 1944-45, the well equipped private in the Army wanted a good pair of Ray-Ban sunglasses, a Zippo lighter, a package of Lucky Strikes and a tailored uniform. All else was secondary. Smoking was encouraged. When in the field, a break was called, "Take 5 and light 'em up," was the standard phrase spoken by the noncom in charge.

Postmark Fayetteville, N.C., May 22, 1944, 12M. Letter dated May 22-44, 8:30 AM, Monday, Fayetteville.

Dearest Mom,

Everything went just about as scheduled & I'm just hanging around the bus station waiting for the mayor of Fayetteville to wake up & unroll the sidewalks. I've got to get a few things, go to the show then go out to camp & "sneak" in without the first Sgt. seeing me--maybe I'll have the rest of the day off.

I'm rather tired but I enjoyed the trip a little. We ran over a Negro down in Ala. Sat. night. He was drunk & the bus driver didn't see him until it was too late so he "straddled" him. Didn't hurt him except for his mental stability. We found him walking down the road--said that someone had tried to run over him.

Say, I forgot to return Mrs. Johnson's (*neighbor at Brady*) thermos bottles--do you mind. Apologize for me not returning them--I forgot all about them.

Tell Ola "hello" for me & write--I see they've just unrolled the sidewalks.

Love, Bud

Evidently I had just returned on the bus from a furlough to Brady, Texas. Many question the fact that I took the bus on this long trip to and from Fayetteville, N.C. to Brady, Texas, rather than riding the train, a faster and better choice of transportation at that time. The truth is I didn't know enough about trains, but was well acquainted with buses.

After the bus ran over the Negro, I suppose I left the bus to help search for the victim and talked to him, however, I do not remember this incident, but I should as it certainly would have been an unusual event.

It was a time, in the forties and much later, before de-segregation, with the "people of color" having separate waiting rooms at the bus station or train depot. There were separate drinking fountains and the balconies at the movie theaters were reserved for the people of color. At Cobb's Drug Store in Brady, the Mexican-Americans were not served at the counter, so to obtain a triple-ice cream cone the children waited at the end of the counter and, when they obtained their cone, went outside to eat. This was an unwritten arrangement that was understood by all and, though wrong, no attempt was made to change the age old customs.

One day in 1943, we had a full house of people lined up at the counter of Cobb's Drug Store in Brady, which seated perhaps fifteen. The bus had just arrived from wherever and filled the fountain with both the counter seating and the booths being full. One of the persons seated at the counter was an young Hispanic man wearing a uniform and I surmised he had a short layover from his bus trip. I told him,"We did not serve ...." I spoke without thinking and he did not allow me to finish, getting off the counter's stool and going toward the door. I realized then, for the first time, what a disgrace the unwritten law had become and how rash I had been in my action.

I called, "Wait." But the damage was done. Those customers at the counter who had overheard my conversation, expressed the same shame which I felt. I could not run after him, though I wished I could, and there is no question that I should have. I was seventeen years old, being raised with many unwritten laws, and knew no better. I learned a lot that day at the soda fountain counter in Cobb's Drug Store.

After the war was over, Mother and Dad purchased a book for me which listed all of the service men who came from McCulloch County, Texas (Brady was the county seat). All of the armed force men were listed alphabetically and I found my name and picture in the "Ls." At the end of the list and pictures of service men, after the "Zs," were the three African-Americans who served from McCulloch County, segregated in the book as they were most every where else: Joseph Daniel Mason, Robert Ellis Menefield, and Frank Stanfield. Each of these African-American soldiers served overseas and became non-coms.

While on furlough to Brady, I was very careful to not use some of the graphic language which we used as a matter of course in the Army, a bad habit I had acquired along with the majority of the rest of the Army, it seemed. Mother would have fallen from her chair if I had asked, "Mother, would you please pass the blankety-blank sugar?" Fortunately I did not make such a faux pas.

Postmark Fort Bragg. N.C., May 24, 1944, 10 AM. Letter dated May 23-44, Tues., 4:15 PM. Return address: Co. F, 397th Inf., Apo 447, Ft. Bragg, N.C.

Dearest Mom,

Gee, I was glad to hear from you--it was a very sweet letter, lady. I need to apologize too--I should have kept the hat--I regretted having given it away afterwards--but I had opened my mouth--stuck both feet in it. I think that I'd better buy you a new hat (Stetson, of course). You're really the best & only gal I need.

(*This referred to a hat that the family had given me. I do not recall the exact circumstances, but I ended up giving it to a girl that I knew who had admired the hat. It did look good on her. I was criticized for giving the hat away, justifiably so.*)

Everything was about the same upon my arrival--naturally there has been some disorder & corruption because I left, that's to be expected. I had a lot of mail waiting--Jean wrote a long letter with check book--just threw it in the waste basket. I'm about broke but don't use much here so will get along.

We're going out in the field to stay all tomorrow night--just got through getting everything ready--never can get everything done.

It's really hot here now hasn't rained since I left except for a sprinkle this afternoon. We were out for a BN. review--there was only one cloud in the sky & we got our khakis damp from a shower & sweat. It'll probably really rain tomorrow night.

Write me. All my love, Bud

I wish I had stayed over until late Friday night & seen the graduation--I can see that I could have now but you never can tell. I'm getting back into the swing of things now (one day) & seems like I hadn't had a furlough at all. I was, I'll have to admit, rather homesick yesterday & last night. I'll live OK.

Postmark Fort Bragg, N.C., May 27, 1944, 11:30 AM. Letter dated May 25-44, 4:00 PM, Thurs.

Dearest Mom,

I've been pretty busy--we went out in the field yesterday at noon & stayed 24 hours. I had to sleep on the cold, cold, ground--only it wasn't cold--it was hot as heck all day. Had us worried last night--clouded up & looked like it was going to drown us but surprisingly it didn't even sprinkle until this afternoon after we got back in camp then we really had to swim for it! I was on K.P. in the field--dirty work.

I just got cleaned up about chow time..feel good now.

I'm strictly G.I now--takes about two days to get used to the routine, etc. I'll live.

Friday--

I just got in from the show--pretty good murder mystery. I'm sorta tired. I've been on the go & yet haven't done anything.

I've been up most of the afternoon being interviewed for a transfer within the regt., so may have a slight change of address. That is, if they want me--it was voluntary & I can't swim so I don't know for sure as yet. It's more scouting & patrolling. I'll like it if I can get in.

I picked up a 75mm shell the other day--it's perfectly safe--the cap was lying separate of the case or I wouldn't have dared handle it. I'll send it home as soon as I find something to put it in. It's an old rusty one but I'd like to have it at home.

I've got a good book here to curl up with so will say....Love, Bud

Say, you may not realize it & I didn't before I got in this man's Army, but it's really nice to have a home to tie to--especially a swell one like I have...Bud

I have no idea what happened to the 75mm shell casing which I sent home. Since Dad was not interested in home decorating I doubt that it ended up as a flower holder, or as a conversation piece on the mantle. I would guess Mother gradually moved it from where ever it was to the garage, then to the trash. Believe it or not, garage sales had not been invented in the early or mid-forties.

Postmark Fort Bragg, N.C., May 29, 1944, 10 AM. Letter dated May 27-44, Sun., 1:00 PM.

Dearest Mom,

I'm over at the guardhouse now loafing--no I didn't try to desert or anything--I'm on guard. I haven't walked guard much so far about five hours but am awfully sleepy & without ambition. I slept all morning but it's awfully hot & a few flies & the heat can make a guy feel awful.

I just got back from the mess hall--had a good dinner--fried chicken--mashed potatoes--gravy--buttered beets--tomato & lettuce salad--hot buns--& ice cream.

About the pictures--just send the prints & let me see if there is anything worth going to the trouble of getting the negatives for. And be sure & tell me how much they are so I can send you the money. It'll have to be about the 15th though as I won't be paid until then on the supplementary payroll. No, I don't need any money thanks anyway (you're awfully sweet to me) I'll have to be self sustaining.

This old Army life will be right down Lee's line (*Lee Shannon, another first cousin)* --hope he gets a good deal--I wish we could be together--he'd make a good scout.

Tell Ola "hello", etc for me. How did the teeth go, OK?

Write... Love, Bud

There is a note on the outside, front of the envelope, "Hi! Ernest!." Might it be possible that "Ernest" was the mail carrier at Brady? This could certainly be the case as Brady was a small town and everybody knew everybody else and the car in which they rode into town.

Postmark Fort Bragg, N.C., May 31, 1944, 10 AM. Letter is dated May 30-44, 9:15 PM, Tues.

Dearest Mom,

Just a short note to let you know that I'm OK & everything's fine. We've been working a little harder--was out all last night & have been cleaning up equipment today.

Laundry service is a little bad so I had to wash a stack of underwear--my pride is greatly hurt.

I'm sending the pictures home--except for a couple--keep around--put in my photo book or something. I haven't time to do any photographic work so put the negs. up where they'll keep will ya?

I told you that I had had some portraits made here at the P.X. They were mailed on the 15th of May to you. You should have them by now--if you don't get them by the 5th let me know. If you do get them & they're any good--give one to Ola, Shorty and keep one yourself. If they're not any good throw them away.

Bud

If I don't sound so jubilant tonight it's because my morale is a little low--maybe it was the corny show I saw tonight. "Gaslight" was here a few days ago--see it if you can, it's really good--that is, the acting is good (Bergman especially)!

Postmark Fort Bragg,, N.C., June 2, 1944, 11:30 AM. Letter dated June 1-44, Payday!

Dearest Mom,

Was on table waiters tonight--just got off--took a cold shower & find that my morale is extremely high--couldn't be because I got some mail--letter from you & Shorty--hooray!

Ah, I'll bet Ola looked pretty with hardly any (or is it "no") teeth. Kendall is still working hard I guess--two bucketfuls of water isn't much--He may have had to carry it both ways if from a stream--field sanitation rules or something--of course he had to make two trips with one bucket..see

(*I drew a picture of a stick figure that was supposed to represent Kendall, cousin, making trips with a bucket of water to a clothes line for 1/4 mile each direction. I have no memory of what this was all about. Kendall was in the Air Corps and perhaps was in Africa by now)*

Yes, see that those pictures get disbursed--one to you--Ola--& Shorty--if there's a small one like you say do what you want with it. How much were those 35mm films? I want to send you the money for them (when I get paid the 10th)! I sent those prints back. About those of Kendall's--I sent them you know just before I left--they weren't sent back or anything--

didn't you get them?
Nothing much to write--going out on the carbine range tomorrow. Will write more later.
Love, Bud

12M. Letter dated June 3-44, 5:45 PM, Sat.
Postmark Fort Bragg, N.C., June 4, 1944
Dearest Mom,
I just got back from chow (early on Sats.)-attended mail call--the important function of the day. Much to my dismay I had none. After all what can I expect--I've been neglecting you. Sorry, Lady, it won't happen again!
I rummaged through a box of stationery here in my foot locker & guess what I found--a letter to you written before my furlough with Kendall's pictures--joke's on me! I'll send them but not the letter--it's rather stale by now, yes?
Lewis--one of the guys in the platoon--wanted to go out on pass but had table waiters tomorrow so we got together for a nominal fee and arranged for him to go anyway. This also relieves me from my former financial state of being "flat" broke.
I'm perched on the edge of the bunk on my left with nothing but a brief on--it's awfully hot--we've been taking salt tablets & working like little dogs. I'm afraid that I didn't do so good out on the carbine transition range. I just barely qualified. It takes all of your shots to find out how your rifle's shooting--I'll do better next time.
Write me... Love, Bud

We were issued Garand M1 rifles, the standard for

the armed forces in WWII. It was a great rifle, holding eight rounds in a clip that automatically ejected when empty with the magazine staying open ready to receive a new clip. It certainly could not compare to the German "Burp Gun," which had a high rate of fire, faster than the Army's .30 caliber machine guns.

The problem with the M1 was its weight. It weighed almost ten pounds or so, so I looked upon the smaller carbine with envy. Unfortunately they were only issued to officers, non-coms and perhaps a few others. Not to a regular G.I. like myself.

Postmark Fort Bragg, N.C., June 6, 1944, 9:20 PM. Father's day card published by Olde Quill Studios, Chicago #25FD1. Has picture of trout lake, fisherman in mountain setting. No date on card to Dad.

Pater, come payday I'll dig you up something that might be useful to you--until then this will have to suffice.

Anyway, next time I come home we'll go deer hunting, yes? I'll bring my M1 to show you a real rifle.

Postmark Fort Bragg, N.C., June 6, 1944, 12M. Letter dated June 5, Mom night 9:00 PM.

Dear Mom,

Was very surprised & pleased to get a box of those butter tarts after chow--naturally having eaten rather heavily as usual I really feel like I've had a heavy meal after eating three or four of those.

They're good & thanks. A few of the other guys managed to get in on them too--"delicious"--unquote!

Also got short note on large greeting card--rather impersonal but was better than nothing.

Haven't done anything all day & consequently we all feel rather sluggish. I went to see a couple of training films this afternoon & that's all. On top of that I'd seen one--the old Army "Mickey Mouse of the training films"-about 8 or 10 times--quite boring after the first three times.

Ah, at last--it cooled off--went to bed with bad case of "bunk fatigue" & found myself under a blanket & still cold--it's wonderful for a change.

Some of the lucky individuals in our Regt. are privileged by going to N.Y. for an Infantry parade--no, Lindsey always gets the raw end of the deal so he doesn't go--guess they figured that I'd ruin the review by staring at the tall buildings in a true country hick manner instead of marching at attention.

Just took an invigorating cold shower--had to--must be the fireman's night off.

Night & love, Bud

Each barracks had a fireman assigned (one of the G.I.s) during colder weather whose job was to keep the boiler for the water fired. I do not remember how it was fired...maybe it was coal??

I don't remember what the "butter tarts" were, but they must have been a favorite dessert around our house. Mother probably made these out of pie crust dough, with sugar and cinnamon. And of course, with real butter. Oleomargarine was available, but was not generally used. Later, at the time "Oleo" became a household word, there was a big controversy about adding color to the Oleo. Until this matter was solved, the housewife had to purchase a pound of Oleo without coloring, adding her own color with a separate package of coloring which accompanied her purchase.

Postmark Fort Bragg, N.C., June 10, 1944, 10 AM. Letter dated June 9-44, Fri, 8:30 PM

Dearest Mom,

I got a nice long letter from you after evening chow--thanks!

There's really nothing new. I wrote Jean at noon--we've been out on a big bare sandy field practicing this afternoon--you can really sweat sometimes.

Makes you feel good to get hot & dirty then come in & take a good shower--maybe it'll work off my "pot belly" I've developed by eating too much.

I don't know how much time off we'll get at Wilson but we'll all have fun--something different anyway! I think we'll have a dance one night--hope we don't have to sleep in pup tents!

Yes! I liked Betty's pictures--they look a little more grown up than Betty really is but have had lots of compliments on them.

About the time I get to know the guys in the barracks pretty well, I move. I don't know when as yet but I'll have to move about 500 yards down by the P.X. It's a lot of trouble--don't know whether it's worth it or not!

Lewis (sleeps on my left--from Mass.) isn't around to bother me tonight so it's sorta lonesome. We're always clowning around. One of the guys gave me a hot foot the other day while I was asleep & it took me a couple of seconds too long to wake up--got a blister. Some times we get industrious & put sand in one of the guy's beds or loosen his springs & tie them with string. Maybe we get a balloon & fill with water or place a helmet liner with water over his bed.

Night, Lady...write Shorty & go to bed.

Love, ya, Bud

P.S. The invasion finally got under way didn't it? We're here looking forward to it & following it with a lot of interest (naturally)--it'll be slow--but sure. Bud

It's interesting to note that the news of the D-Day invasion of France only rated a "P.S." Seeing this letter fifty-five years later amazes me that I did not write a very lengthy letter about D-Day, an event which certainly affected everyone's lives.

A standard G.I. "hot foot" was accomplished by finding someone asleep with their boots on. You placed a paper, or kitchen match, between the sole and side of their boot and light it. Care was taken to not burn the barracks down. Another trick was to find a G.I. asleep with one arm falling off of the bunk. A helmet was filled with water and lifted under the dangling hand. Theoretically the sensation of the hand in the water caused the sleeping man to wet his pants. Some say it worked, but I cannot testify to the fact as I never was a recipient of the trick, lucking out.

Postmark Fort Bragg, N.C., June 13, 1944, 4:30 PM. Letter dated June 12-44, 11:15 AM.

Return address: Co. F, 397th Inf, APO 447, Ft. Bragg, N.C.

Dearest Mom,

Gee, it's hot & dusty I just got in from practicing for our demonstration up at Wilson--sweating like a Negro. I pulled off my shirt & stepped in shower room & cooled off from the waist up. My trousers are filthy with N.C. fine dust--we may get the afternoon off to straighten up--hope so. We go up in the morning to Wilson--don't know how much time off we'll have--not much I guess.

I got a letter from you & Betty & Tabby--both yesterday--you two should get together on what you write. I told Lewis that I guess I'd get a letter from M.E. in a day or so also telling about the cats almost drowning! No, kidding though I enjoy getting them an awfully lot.

Oh, yes, the slides--there's a supply store here in town--I'll see if I can get a Kodacolor viewer--tell Jean not to bother. Also <u>don't</u> send them to me--I'll see them some other time--I guess. That magnifying glass is in that big trunk on the top layer with all of my darkroom equip.--dig it out but don't lose it.

Must run--more later. Love, Bud

One of the duties which we drew, other than KP (kitchen police), was the guarding of the WAAC's barracks at night. You could compare this arrangement to hiring a fox to guard a hen house. There was supposed to be no talking to the females, but, in spite of all the officer of the guard could do, it happened and romances blossomed.

Postmark Fort Bragg, N.C., June 20, 1944, 12M. Letter dated June 19-44, Monday, 7:15 PM. The return address is now Regt. Hq. Co., 397 Inf. APO 447, Ft. Bragg, N.C.

Dear Pater,

I'm sitting "Indian fashion" on my bunk--it's pretty cool upstairs here this evening. It's cloudy out & looks like a good old summer storm but hasn't rained as yet. Wish it'd rain all night--you can't even tell it's rained two hours after it stops here--sand!

Glad to hear from you--how about that new line. Try it!

You can always go back to what you're doing. If you need any money, I have some war bonds that are yours for the asking. You'll never get anywhere by not trying.

The reference to a "line" probably deals with the profession of Dad's. Since the war started Singer sewing machines were unavailable, forcing him to seek some other line of work. This probably refers to his selling Moor Mans' line of mineral supplements for livestock. The letter continues...

This old Army life is doing me some good--I'm getting brown as a Mex. from going swimming and developing a little muscle. This new Co. is OK so far. I think I'll like it despite previous deductions. Our Platoon sgt. thinks he's really an old Army man. Of course I'm not one to talk--but he's only about 26. He's sorta muscle bound & likes to show it by wearing us down--but he's good!

I was on table waiters today--there isn't much to do--only a small company & good chow, too.

You'd better hang on to that fishing equipment--just because they aren't biting now is no reason to become pessimistic & sell out. There's some good fishing here also & someday if I can make connections I'll get a weekend pass & go up state somewhere.

Write me, Pater. So long for now, Bud

P.S. It looks like it is going to rain after all---hooray!

P.S. Say, ask Mary Ellen to see if she still has a harmonica (mouth organ) of mine--if so & is not using it how about sending it--would appreciate it, But If she doesn't have it in her stuff it's probably out in that box of electrical equip. of mine--probably can't find it. Love, Bud

Having the Company Commander, a Captain, who was twenty-six years of age may seem young now, but at the time it was old. If this twenty-six year old person had been a Private, and being that old, we would have called him "Pop." Of course, we had no inclination to call the Company Commander "Pop."

The barracks at Fort Bragg were double story and the I & R platoon was in the second story of one. It was rumored the parachute trainees would simply jump out of the upper story door rather than go down the stairs, a jump of some fifteen feet.

The Headquarters Company of the 397th Regiment was located at the very end of the barracks area, and, just over the hill, through some woods was Pope Field, the air field. They conducted glider pilot training and sometimes the motor less aircraft landed erroneously in the woods near our barracks.

The food at the Regimental Headquarters mess hall was the best Army food I had experienced before or after. The cooks certainly were talented.

Postmark Fort Bragg, N.C.. Jul 13, 1944, 4:30 PM. Letter dated July 11-44, Monday PM 7:30

Dear Mater,

It looks like the rainy season has firmly established its self in North Carolina--luckily I have tapered off on the salt tablets so as not to unduly endanger myself being dissolved further. I stay so wet that mosquito eggs are laid, hatched, & develop into the larva state in stagnate puddles on my body without being hampered--every night when I come in I have to yell, "quick Henry the Flit!"

Wed. PM, 12:30

Hi Lady, you see what kind of a guy you have for a son--here it is Wed & still trying to finish this letter.

I got the two boxes--cookies were really good. Thanks Betty! The other stuff was just what I wanted (including lemon drops & caramels) thanks--I'll take the rest of those snaps, develop them & send you some--if I don't ruin the roll.

Went out last night on a compass problem--

naturally it led through thickest brush & deepest swamp on the whole post. We all got good & wet--it's a wonder that we didn't get lost, too.

I was leading the patrol on the last azimuth reading & it was really dark. We were down in a swampy low ground & could hardly see each other--I came up to the bank of a little creek. I told the guy behind me that it was only 6 in. deep & 1 1/2 ft across. I forgot to tell him that the water itself was 6 in deep & the banks were about 3 ft high. I stepped across & heard the others come on across until the last man--he missed. I heard some floundering around & strong words--he finally emerged. We had a lot of fun. Wiegel walked off into a foxhole then stuck his head up & said, "Hey boys--guess what? A foxhole."

I have to brush off my trusty M1, so will run--have to stand a division review this afternoon--nutz.

Love, Bud

While at Ft. Bragg we could generally obtain passes to go into Fayettville, the nearest town. Of course Fayettville had become a typical army post town with businesses which catered to the lonesome G.I. If you got off of the main part of town and into some of the old residential areas, it was a charming place with homes built of southern architecture.

There was a nice USO where they had a darkroom which could be scheduled for use if you didn't mind waiting.

North Carolina has liquor rationing which was not

a problem as the majority of us young GIs did not drink except for an occasional beer. However, one Saturday night we all pooled our ration stamps and loose change and two of us went into Fayettville and purchased a quart of rum. The selection of the two who were to make the trip to the liquor store was determined by checking the available volunteers and choosing the two who looked the oldest as you were supposed to be twenty-one to purchase liquor. None of our group were twenty-one. I was selected to be one of the "shoppers" as I had a gray streak in my hair and looked more mature than most others.

When we arrived at the liquor store and stood at the counter inspecting the various bottles, I was careful to remove my cap to expose my hair with the gray.

Not knowing much about the liquor business and even less about the merits of rum, bourbon, blended whiskey, gin and other spirits, we more than likely chose rum because of its lower price and the attractiveness of the bottle and label. Or perhaps, we because liked the song, "Rum And Coca Cola."

We carried our purchase back to the barracks and those who were in that evening proceeded to devour the contents, laced with Coca Cola. It seemed like a lot of fun at the time, but the next morning I, along with many of the others, decided drinking rum was not our thing.

Postmark: Jul 24, 1944, Fort Bragg, N.C.
Return address; Hg. Co., 397th Inf. APO447
Letter dated July 22, -044, 9:30 PM (Air mail...8¢)
Dearest M.E. (*Letter was to little sister, Mary Ellen)*

Haven't had much time to write last few days — can't read my letters very well anyway can you? I've adopted a new technique — I take a blank sheet of paper, spill some ink on it, put it in an envelope and you can say that you've heard from me.

No, I finished the series of tests for Expert Inf. badge last night — passed them all — guess I was just lucky mostly. I'll get that pretty little piece of tin one of these days soon as we have a Bn. (*battalion)* review.

Like I say, I was out late last night on the test (night compass course) so almost didn't even get up for noon chow today. Sorta hard on the old chassis and nerves.

I pulled out my wallet tonight at the show ("Christmas Holiday" — no good) and my harem section (pictures of beautiful gals, etc.) fell open. Sutton, the guy I was with, wanted to know who the good looking gal was. Said she looked sorta young for me. It was (one that you sent me without the dog on dress) picture of you. So, I explained that you were my little sis of whom I was very proud, etc.

I'll bet that you and Shirley did have a good time — you two get along pretty well. I guess I told you that Jack was taking Marine boot training out at San

Diego. Haven't heard from him in two or three weeks. Maybe he passed out.

I also heard from Woodrow at Camp Wallace (guess I mentioned him, too, though). Heard from Bill Merrick (remember him?) — he'll probably be up one of these weekends to Brady, I mean). Tell Polly (Alvie) to be sure & see him & show him around — & tell him "hello" from me, etc.

& you be good and write, Bud

Postmark Fort Bragg, N.C., Jul 25, 1944, 11:30 Am. Letter dated July 23-44, Mom, 8:00 PM

Dearest Mom,

Just a note tonight--wanted to send you Chandler's letter (*"Chandler" is Kendall...his middle name*) & let you know that I am still kicking.

What's this about a fire in the garage--Pater piddling around? None hurt I hope--I saw the notice in the good old Brady Standard. Ahem! I saw my name in one that I got tonight. Oh, yes, I get around.

Feet are kinda tender--had to walk to work instead of riding 16 miles in all--haven't been on a good hike in about six weeks.

This is short--write more when more happens.

Love ya, Bud

Postmark Fort Bragg, N.C., Jul 31, 1944, 10 AM. Letter dated Jul 30-44, 8:30, Sun PM. Return address ASN38559376, Regt. Hq Co. 397 Inf, APO 447, Ft. Bragg, N.C.

Dear Pater,

Haven't had much time to write--working pretty hard the last week. We (just the Platoon) (*This was the I & R --Intelligence & Reconnaissance platoon)* went out in the field for three days last week & when we go out by ourselves we can have plenty of fun. Did everything from studying habits of N.C. ticks & mosquitoes to swiping watermelons out of a corn field.

You know that mineral deal sounded a little unsubstantial at first but from the sound of your letter I think you're selling me, too. Maybe it's a safer past time than throwing matches in trays of gasoline, yes?

This must be in reference to a fire in the garage in Brady and to Dad's starting to sell MoorMan's Minerals for livestock. MoorMan's headquarters are and were in Comanche, Texas. Dad became an advocate of the mineral supplement for cattle and made many friends among the cattle raisers in Central Texas by his efforts. The MoorMan's Company also packaged mineral supplements for humans and Mother also became a fan, taking the product daily. I suppose it was certainly a healthy activity as she lived to be over ninety years old.

The letter continues...

Speaking of fires, you'd better keep an eye on the wiring in the wash house. You'd better change those fuses to a weaker caliber so they'll blow easier in case something happens.

A couple of guys & I went into town last night to use the darkroom at one of the U.S.O.s I developed that roll of film that Betty sent me in my camera--over-developed them a little but maybe O.K. anyway.

I'm sending a box home with some extra stuff in it that I'd better get rid of--it's just in my way--that is, I'll send it as soon as I can lug it over to A.P.O. 447. There's a little wool knit cap that we wear under our helmets that would look cute on Mary Ellen this winter.

Funny things happened while we were out in the field. We tried a river crossing with full equipment then built floats out of our shelter halves, etc.--wet, but fun. One of the guys dropped his rifle & most of his other equipment in about 8 ft. of water--we fished the rifle out but lost about everything else. I'd like to tell you all about this ole stuff the next time I see you--too much to write down.

Looks like it's going to rain again--bit wet.

Love, Bud

P.S. There's two things that I haven't been able to figure out about N.C.--the infantile paralysis & its sales tax---most confusing. We're restricted from going to some counties here because of the Polio.

For some reason I just never got around to learning to swim as a teenager. Oh, I could dog-paddle around staying within easy reach of the bank or shallow water, but that was the extent of my talent. When we were practicing the river crossing while working out in the field beyond the normal boundaries of Ft. Bragg, I didn't worry much about not being able to swim. We all were carrying back packs which would keep you afloat even though each of us carried an eight-pound M1 rifle and some other hardware. We would jump in the deep water and float down river with the current to some shallow rapids.

Post mark Fort Bragg, N.C., Aug 5, 1944, 11:30 AM. Letter dated Aug 2-44, 9:45 PM

Dearest Mater,

Lady, I'm getting pretty bad here--getting to where I write "Shorty" more often than you--Bad! Of Course that's not really say anything--we've been awfully busy--not much time off.

Makes a guy feel pretty good to be busy--appreciates what time he has off. We've been having a little fun though--found a liquor still while on a patrol the other afternoon. I was waiting at a crossroad waiting to direct the chow truck down to our location when a little N.C. future farmer came speeding by on a bike. I told him about finding the still that afternoon--he volunteered the information that the country side was spotted with the things. Also sent scouts to reconnoiter watermelon patches on some of our patrols--we actually buy some once in a while. Don't get the wrong impression of the platoon--there aren't many of us--a little against Army regulations (field manual 21-100) but good!

You mentioned overseas--it's rather inevitable you must realize. Mom, don't worry about this G.I.--he knows how to take care of himself--knows himself more than you or anyone does so won't lead with my chin.

This old overseas duty wouldn't necessarily mean too much either & it's a ways off, also. Don't let it bother you--need to see the world anyway--have something to tell my grand children.

Got Mary Ellen's letter (the sensible one) the

other day--I'll write her & tell her all about the N.C. watermelons when we get in day after tomorrow.

Say, let's stay in Texas--it's something to be from the old state--everybody wants to touch you!

Getting late...night, Bud

The I & R Platoon, while in the field, worked in areas which were outside of Fort Bragg. There were farms mostly with tobacco crops. I had never seen this type of agriculture and it was interesting to me. The small log drying huts for the tobacco leaves were full of the recent harvest with the leaves hanging from their ceilings.

Postmark Fort Bragg, N.C., Aug 18, 11:30 AM. Letter is via air mail & has 8¢ Air Mail stamp. Letter is dated Aug 17-44, Thurs, 9:00 PM.

Dear Pop,

I haven't really anything to write about in particular. I've been living about the same old dismal existence. Went out this afternoon & learned how to use tree climbers & safety harness. How's the mineral sales going? I haven't heard very much from anybody the last week or so--been too darn busy to write myself. That should be an all season deal--am I right there?

I got my certificate to wear the Expert Inf. badge but the old Army's a little slow in presenting that little badge--guess I'll have to buy myself one. It's quite a fancy--the whole thing -- $5 is $5.

We had our first training under cover of artillery

(live) the last couple of weeks--good experience. I like to hear those 105s go over. OK as long as they keep going!

Gonna rain here tonight--nice cool breeze streaming in--starting to rain.

'night, Bud

Part of the basic training and beyond was being able to use the pole climbing equipment which was placed on each foot, the same type of equipment which a utility company person would use to climb a utility pole to make repairs. This type of training would allow the soldier to repair existing communication lines or to install new lines. Of course, part of the equipment was a safety belt.

Postmark Fort Bragg, N.C., Sep 4, 1944, 11:30 AM. Letter dated Sept 3-44, Sunday, 9:30 AM

Dearest Mom,

Today I am as nearly a physical wreck as a guy could be. I just got in last night from a pass. Sutton couldn't get a plane to Chicago so he went with me down to the Carolina Beach below Wilmington, N.C. Sutton's a pretty fair sort of a guy--kinda queer (*I didn't mean "queer" as in gay. In 1944-45 we didn't know what a gay was. Perhaps they hadn't been invented as yet)*--but we had a pretty good time running around (*hitchhiking, our standard method of getting from point A to point B*). We stopped by White Lake on the way back & spent most of Sat--it's really a nice place--big lake about 10 miles around it with a crystal sand bottom. No inlets or outlets on it. It's as clear as water could be all the way across it. I took quite a few pictures--I"ll send you some when I get them back. Also met more interesting people (both sexes).

I'm out now east of the regt. area making myself scarce. The smart G.I. (like myself) always gets as far from the barracks as possible on Sundays to keep away from the C.Q.(*Charge of Quarters)* & details.

Thanks for the avalanche of letters from all the relatives & everything--rather have a longer one from you all. Should have some mail--just lots of it today--haven't been to mail call in about three days.

I sent a box by RR Express last Saturday. No doubt, you will have got it or will shortly. I may send for those long handles this winter--they're good.

You won't get anymore bonds from Uncle Sam of mine, I don't think. They've cut out the bond allotments & are selling $10 bonds to us--easier to buy.

I see by ye olde Brady Standard that John Rudder has a new drug store where Stanton's Cafe was--I'll bet it's pretty nice.

Sutton & I met an old gent down on the Carolina Beach that was quite an authority on the Civil War--on the South's side--he was all ready to fight it over with Sutton (Mich.). Personally I think he was too old to have been in the Civil War. Also met a little gal from El Paso...old home week. Love, Bud

This was one of few weekend passes on which I spent the night away from the base. Sutton and I had an enjoyable, but uneventful weekend looking around. We spent the night in some economical hotel. It had to be economical because of necessity.

We did meet a couple of girls at White Lake but nothing came of the meeting. I believe that when the female pair found we were soldiers, they lost interest. We were in bathing suits so they couldn't tell we were in the Army by our dress. It was somewhat encouraging that viewing our bodies as we looked in bathing suits was not the thing which made them lose interest.

Postmark Fort Bragg, N.C., Sep 6, 1944, 12M. Letter dated Sept 6-44, Tues, 9:30 P.M.

Dear Mom,

Here I haven't been doing anything that takes so much of a guy's time & still don't get around to writing. Haven't any definite training schedule so nothing of interest seems to happen anymore.

Pater, I went out this morning to fire a little 45 cal. sub-machine gun. It has a wire stock--collapsible--nice. Made expert--get me one to hunt jackrabbits with--supposed to only cost $7.50. Congrads on your birthday--thought of it but haven't been to town & haven't been broke at the same time--give you a rain check.

More tomorrow, lights out. Love, Bud

Here's a clipping out of Inf. Journal. Glad you think the Ex. Inf. is <u>something</u>--$5 to me--explain it all to you sometime.

The Army's most economical firearm was probably

the little .45 caliber "machine pistol" with the collapsible stock. The magazine held about 15 rounds, but it was rather slow fire compared to the "burp" gun which the German Army used. Because of its physical appearance, the automatic rifle was called the "grease" gun. It was also not very accurate, being best used at close range.

Postmark Fort Bragg, N.C., Sep 13, 1944, 12M. Letter dated Sept 12-44, Tues noon.

Dearest Pater,

I haven't much time before we get put to work doing something. I just wanted to drop a note to enclose my E.I. (*Expert Infantry*) badge cert.--have to get rid of it along with a lot of other stuff--I seem to have acquired a lot of stuff the few months--use some of it if you can. I probably won't have any use for it after the war anyway. I may send for that knife later. It's hard to say how long—there doesn't seem to be any great rush--you know how the old Army operates.

How's the business going--things should be good there after what I saw in the olde Brady Standard about the rain, etc. just now.

Saw some young quail the other day--just could fly. We had a dog out with us on our hike--he flushed a covey of about 15 or 20

Must run, the Sgt. beckons, Bud

I was transferred from the I & R Platoon in the 397th Regimental Headquarters Company to Company E, same regiment, as the company runner. The I & R

Platoon sergeant, Sgt. Peiffer, called me aside one day and explained I was being moved from the platoon. He offered no explanation and I requested none. I hated to be moved from the I & R platoon as it turned out I hardly got to know any of the members of Company E, my new company. Some years after the war I corresponded with Corporal James Sweeney of the I & R Platoon's cadre and he advised me that the platoon went through the war with only one casualty, Bernard Brauer.

Sergeant Peiffer was a short fellow, but tough. He strutted around like a bandy rooster with a demeanor which squashed any inclination by the members of the platoon to defy his authority. He had our respect. I heard later, after the war, Peiffer was given a battlefield commission.

We were moved, as a division, to Camp Kilmer, New Jersey preparing to board a ship for Europe, the exact destination unknown.

We did obtain passes to go into New York with, I think, transportation being provided by Army busses. I took a tourist's tour, gawking at the tall buildings, several stories taller than those in Fort Worth and unheard of heights in Brady, Texas.

I went to a movie in a very large movie theater

which featured the movie *Kismet*, a new feature at that time, starring Ronald Coleman and Marlene Dietrich. I don't remember the plot of the movie but I do remember Marlene had nice legs, an enlarged picture of which was prominently displayed on a billboard over the theater.

I was not about to venture onto New York City's subway system. I had no idea how they worked or where they went and if I did get on one, I would not know how to get back. I certainly missed an opportunity to explore that great city.

I did not go to the Empire State Building, but did see Times Square. I ate lunch at an "automat," the first such a facility I had seen, certainly a far cry from the soda fountain at Cobb's Drug in Brady. You put your nickels and quarters in slots by the little windows displaying slices of pie, sandwiches and other food. I was awed by this more than I was awed by the tall buildings. You then took your tray to a table and enjoyed your meal. I sat at a table and was joined shortly by a civilian fellow who asked me if the Yankees had won the game that afternoon. Of course, I had no idea, but did guess that he referred to the World Series, of which I was vaguely aware.

It turned out the Yankees did win the series in 1943 about the time that we sailed overseas on the

George Washington, a former luxury liner which was part of the reparations assessed the German Government for World War I.

It was interesting to me to find that this ship transported a German citizen from Europe to America about 1925, a German who was not on the passenger list — a stowaway. This person was Bruno Richard Hauptman who was convicted and executed for the kidnapping and death of Charles and Anne Lindbergh's infant son in 1936.

The George Washington was built in 1908 and was 723 feet long and 72 feet wide and there were G.I.s in every foot of her space.

We sailed from New York on October 6, 1944, some five days after my nineteenth birthday.

CHAPTER FIVE

OVERSEAS

The trip to our destination, Marseilles, France, took about ten days and was an experience never to be forgotten by a Central Texas just-turned-nineteen-year old who had not been further from home than Carlsbad, New Mexico. I stayed on deck whenever I could, watching the flying fish and the dolphins (or porpoises) racing along with the ship. At night the phosphorescence in the salt water waves at the bow of the George Washington was like a light show. Chow was two times a day with an unvaried menu with SOS (s.... on shingle) being the main entree for breakfast, lunch and dinner. Actually the chow line was constant, with each company being assigned a time to eat.

There was a perpetual crap game going of which I did not participate. Not only did I not want to, I had no knowledge of such a type of game where you kneel on a blanket and talk to the dice in pleading terms.

We were traveling in a convoy consisting of many ships including an aircraft carrier. I knew nothing about the sea and boats as my experience was limited to a twelve foot rowboat on a dirt tank (people north of the Mason-Dixon line refer to them as "ponds") or Brady Creek in McCulloch County, Texas. When the convoy ran through a hurricane in the Atlantic, I had no idea of the concept of hurricanes. Tornadoes, yes. Hurricanes, no. I could still go on deck, with the wind howling, and would look, it seemed to me, up at the towering waves. I could look across the water, when we were on top of a wave, and see the aircraft carrier topping a crest with its prop out of the water.

Amazingly I did not get seasick during the storm, or before. Most of the passengers spent a lot of time being sick and were unable to eat. I did feel queasy, but did not get sick. I didn't eat much because of the queasy stomach. Of course the menu of only one entree′ was a deterrent to eating. For a landlocked person with no experience, it was very, very educational.

This late in the war the German U-Boats were less of a threat, though we did not know this. After we moved away from the storm area the voyage was uneventful. As we entered the Mediterranean Sea, during the daylight hours, I had a chance to see the Rock of Gibraltar on our left, a famous landmark only previously seen in magazines.

Postmark U.S. Army, 20th Base PO, Oct 21, 1944. Has censor's stamp #45820, R.P. Schmidt, 2nd Lt.. Return address is Co E, 397 Inf., APO 447, c/o P.M, NY, N.Y. Letter dated Oct. 23-44, Somewhere in France. (written in pencil)

Dearest Mom,

As it so happens, there isn't a Railway Express office around close--so I guess you'd better mark that Angel food cake up to profit & loss--mostly loss! There are a couple of things that I need rather badly. I wish you'd box that hunting knife & wool scarf & a woolen undershirt up and send them--that's all I really need--if there are any spare corners left over for some of those good home made cookies that Bets put out they'd really hit the spot.

I started a couple of letters on the boat but didn't get around to finishing them--not that I was too busy. It was sort of a pleasure cruise--nothing to do but eat & sleep. They did have a show every day in what they called the "little theater" -- it was on one of the hatches that was partially enclosed to produce semi-darkness & seating (& standing) room for about 50 of the lucky ones who could get in. By the time one show had finished, there would be a five deep ring around the hatch waiting to get in. At the end of each showing there followed a mad free for all--those on the inside trying to get out & those trying to get in--complete with stretcher bearers standing by. But all that danger of being crushed is past now--all I have to watch for now is keeping from being drowned--so wet that the ducks carry umbrellas.

Ask Betty to straighten out my address with the Standard--look forward to that paper. Should have some mail in today--hope so. Will send that insurance money even if I have to send Francs. Must close--using up my daily paper ration--have to use it for <u>lots</u> of things now.

Been to *(here a rectangle had been cut out of the paper by the censor as I gave the name of the place in France)* --rustic place. Love, Bud

My sister, Betty, worked for the Brady newspaper while she was in high school and continued employment at the paper after she graduated.

After disembarking at Marseilles our division was marched to a point a few miles north of the seacoast town. We were housed in tents, but a semipermanent, multi-station latrine had been built of wood, with no top, sides nor doors above a pit. Using this not-so-private facility, with civilians walking by not 100 yards away, was disconcerting but I finally got more comfortable with this as I learned that in France during wartime such a thing was readily accepted. It was nothing to be in an open transport truck and pass a female relieving herself along side the road in broad daylight. Another cultural shock was to find that the men's urinals in Marseilles were merely barriers on the street that covered the user from the knees up to his shoulders. No doubt the architect of these urinals had in mind the user being able to tip his hat to the ladies as they passed by.

V-Mail, postmark U.S. Army Postal Service, Nov 5, 1944, 12 PM. Return address, Co E., 397 Inf. APO, c/o P.M., N.Y. NY. letter dated Nov 2 or 3 (?) Censor # 45810

Dearest Mater,

After having proven to myself that while both are appetizing individually, navy beans & butter scotch (G.I.) pudding do not go well together in the same mess kit. I retire to my cozy one-room adobe to let you know that France is still as muddy as it was the last time I wrote--with no hope for it drying out at all.

I was awfully glad to get Dad's letter with yours--I'll write to him tomorrow if I have time--it's getting dark now. A guy hasn't got much time to write anymore so don't worry if you don't hear from me.

Love, Bud

Postmark U.S. Army Postal Service, Nov 7, 1944, 12M. Regular letter (not V-Mail) dated France, Nov 4-44, via Air Mail with 8¢ stamp

Dear Pater,

All I have to say is that I don't ever see how I was discontented at jerking sodas--the most beautiful part was lying around in bed until 8:00--'sfunny no matter where I go in this ole Army you always have to get up at daylight--then sit around all day--beats me!

Mom sent me a letter to the family from you--glad you got a good deal. I guess salesmen are a little hard to find. What happened..do you live away from home all of the time? I'll send this to the house--no doubt you'll get it.

This refers to Dad's having to get a job in Louisiana at a factory which was manufacturing parachutes for the Army. After the war started the Singer Company stopped the manufacture of new sewing machines and turned to making products associated with the war effort. I believe Dad was in charge of keeping the sewing machines running and adjusted. I never discussed this part of his life with

Dad, but I guess he kept a room in Louisiana. Going back and forth from Louisiana to Brady, Texas, during war time would have been almost impossible due to the shortage of gasoline and tires for a car. I understand the speed limit was thirty-five miles per hour during WWII, a further hardship. The letter continues...

Seems like I told Mom what a low opinion I had of France in general. Since then, I've seen a little more of it--it's really like a picture postcard in places--grand country. French population is friendly almost anywhere you go--give you wine & fruit--nice people. I guess you know more about it all than I do--you were here longer than I have been. (*Dad was in WWI in France and served in the Field Artillery*)

'Tis one advantage to this rugged life that I'm leading--low overhead & minimum of bathing. I've spent about 4 or 5 dollars the last month--took two salt water showers (on ship)--oh, I brush my teeth every once in a while--wash this pan of mine off & shave--too cold to take baths--good thing there's plenty of fresh air circulating. Besides it's sorta hard to take a tub bath in a steel helmet.

Be glad when the mail catches up with us...write me...

Your offspring, Bud

During our brief stay just outside of Marseilles we did get to go into town. I went to a French movie and had no idea of the plot or its ending as I knew only a couple of words of French which, as far as I could tell, were not used during the 90 minute film. I was surprised to find ushers who insisted on helping you find a seat and who expected to be tipped, an unheard of practice at either of the two theaters in Brady, Texas.

We also climbed a whole bunch of steps to a large Cathedral, entered, lit candles and was asked by a Priest (sign language) if we wanted to give confessions. I declined. After all, at barely nineteen and being raised as I was, I hardly had anything to confess and I was unsure, due to my limited experience, if it would have been necessary to confess to thoughts or just deeds. Thoughts were abundant, deeds were few. Besides all of my family's church going had been to small Baptist and Methodist churches and I was uncomfortable being in a large church of the Catholic faith in a foreign country.

Our division moved out of Marseilles northward in trucks, the route being along the Rhone River valley. The invasion of Southern France near Marseilles had taken place in the middle of August, 1944, by the 36th Division prior to our arrival and the results of the havoc rained upon the defending Germans, as they tried to escape inland, was evident along our route of travel. There were destroyed German vehicles of all types lining each side of the highway, having been pushed off to clear the road. Of course, any bodies had been removed by the time of our trip, but seeing our first clear evidence of warfare, other than in movies, had quite an impact on our minds.

Postmark U.S. Army Postal Service, Nov 10, 1944, 12M. Censor #45820, R.P Schmidt. Letter Nov 8-44

Dear Pater,

My interest in life in general is again renewed. I arose this morning at the usual daybreak hour--it was chilly & raining but needless to say I was quite jubilant for a couple of reasons. Firstly, when I arose (unwillingly), it was from a nice dry, straw-stuffed French mattress in a nice dry French room--too bad that this can't last for the duration, no?

Of course along with the bed, etc., some the house in general full of interesting objects & useful. items besides myself, a few other muddy (& happy) G.I.s, we have three sewing machines--of course two of these are Singers. One in my room is really a good one (new stand)(bobbin in vertical position)--anyway, yesterday morning I got really eager & sewed an extra pocket on the side of my fatigues leg--handy. (*I used the pockets, one on each side, to put grenades*) I seem to collect all kind of junk & when I try to sort it out it is all classed as "essential"--you know how it is.

On top of all this pleasurable environment that has been placed around me--mail came in last night--oh, happy day--glad to hear that your minerals are going OK.

Glad to hear that Ralph (*cousin*) is back & OK--

don't ever hear much from the guys. Ask Mom to write Mrs. Davis & find out what Harold's address is & what outfit he's in--he's probably in France by now--might run across him in my travels.

Yes, 'tis truly a lot of fun sometimes. On thing about this place--we won't starve. There happens to be a garden (carrots, beets, turnips, potatoes) out in back that we are rescuing from the sad future of rotting away. It's rumored that some certain guys had chicken for chow last night--of course I wouldn't go out & kill a poor defenseless chicken & pick & clean him. But, it would be good stuffed with carrots, onions, bouillon powder (G.I.) & potatoes & roasted in convenient pots in still more convenient & appreciated French stoves.

Some of the guys inform me that yesterday was election day--no doubt we have that man again--being a Democrat 'tis OK by me.

Last night my confidence in our humble adobe & in French homes in general was rudely shattered--the roof leaks; but we move from spot to spot just ahead of the flood. I have a nice 3/4 bed all to myself with civilian covers--none too clean but I'm not either--soooo.

Say, tell Mom (everybody in ye olde family) to go ahead & don't hesitate to write on backs of sheets as they naturally don't censor incoming mail--whatever you do, keep writing often.

I don't remember, of course, but the rules prevented the G.I.s from writing on the backs of the sheets of paper on mail back to the states. Writing only on one side of the paper allowed the censor to cut out an unsuitable word or phrase without obliterating the information that might be on the back of the sheet. Letters from home to France were not censored. The letter continues...

A couple of guys are out back looking at a goat with a gleam in their stomachs--better see what's up.
Bud

The town in which we were quartered in French homes was probably Baccarat, France.

We moved up on line about November 7th or 8th relieving some elements of the 45th Division, near St. Helene, France, in the approaches to the Vosges Mountains in southeastern France. My job in Company E, 397th Regiment was the company runner. I stayed close to the company Captain and First Sergeant having the assignments of leading the platoons back to a rear area for hot chow, when it was available, and staying in contact with the company to our front when we were moving. And other duties as they came up. I was never advised of our strategic situation, as I was only advised on a need-to-know basis, a term that had not been invented until later years. Besides, I didn't need to know much to be a company runner.

We received our first fire almost immediately, with the Germans dropping mortar rounds and artillery fire.

Naturally we knew that when we stopped it was prudent to start a foxhole as no one had any idea how long we might be held at a particular location; perhaps 10 minutes, perhaps a full day and night.

Soon after we came on line I saw my first dead German soldier. He was lying on his back along side our route up the gentle slope of a hill. We were curious of him as there was no apparent damage to his body. Even his helmet was correctly in place, his hands beside his side. His uniform was strained tight as the trunk of his body had swelled due to the gasses generated by the starting decomposition of his body even though the weather was cold. The buttons on his blouse were in danger of popping off. His face had a color that I could not describe. There was no way to tell how long he had lain along side our path. In training we were not advised of the problems with warfare such as the removal and burial of the dead, occurrences that were sure to happen.

We dug in. As it turned out we were in this location overnight and I was able to use the dead German as a marker of where to turn to reach our company area. I passed by the dead German several times during the next 24 hours. The next morning there was frost covering his face as the night had been very close to freezing. I'll always remember that dead German soldier, an image forever etched in my mind. It was hard to tell his age. He could have been a teenager, as most of us, or an older man. He surely had a family and would be missed. He was the first dead person I had seen other than in a funeral parlor.

We received quite a bit of German artillery fire in this location and our company suffered its first casualty. One of our men dived for his foxhole but the incoming round hit a tree almost directly over his location and he suffered a fatal wound from shrapnel in his back. For the first time it became clear to me at this time that I could possibly get killed. Prior to that day, I had not given much thought to getting hurt or killed. I, along with most of the others, felt it would happen to someone else, not me. Actually an infantryman lasting the war without getting killed, wounded or captured is rare, a fact which applies to both the good guys and the bad guys.

Later, perhaps a day or two later, we were in a wooded area where three of us shared a foxhole which we dug, found some pine tree branches to construct a top and covered the top with dirt. We placed some pine needles in the bottom to protect us from the damp earth, laid a shelter half down and we were "snug as bugs in a rug." Unfortunately the Germans cared less for our sleep as they released a lot of rounds that night on our positions, including the "screaming meenies," a type of shell that made a terrible sound as it approached designed to rattle the enemy. And they did just that. One round hit just beside our foxhole shattering the stock of one of our occupants' M1 rifle which he had leaned against at tree within reach of our foxhole. Other than the shattered rifle stock, we were showered with dirt and, after our ears stopped ringing, we found ourselves otherwise unhurt. We were learning rapidly a well constructed, deep foxhole was absolutely necessary to our healths.

As the front moved slowly through the rising mountains, I shared another foxhole with one other member of our company. A foxhole which was well constructed, but I had found that the two grenades, one on each side, in my side pockets I had sewn to the sides of my trouser legs prevented me from lying on my side so I hollowed out two cavities in the side of the foxhole and placed the grenades in the cavities. The next morning when we moved out of the area, I forgot the grenades.

••••••••••

After the war I had worried that someone, perhaps a child, might find the grenades and pull their pins. In recent years, after the internet came into use, I received information from a Frenchman, Lionel Humbert, who was born in Raon L'Etape, France, a town in the area of our November operation. His father was the mayor of that French city during the war. After the war Mr. Humbert roamed the battle area as a young man and collected artifacts from the battlefield. He advised me that he had over 100 grenades (unarmed I hope) and uncountable empty clips from the M1 rifle. Lionel Humbert also told of the German soldier bodies being buried in the Vosges without any markers to indicate their graves. The grave sites are routinely found but not all of those buried had dog tags. So, as far as I know, no disasters befell someone as a result of my forgetting the two grenades that morning and it is very possible the two forgotten grenades were found by Lionel Humbert.

••••••••••••••

After only a few days of being on line, I became an expert on foxholes. I found they needed to be deep, narrow and in an area where the Germans would not drop an artillery round. At one place where the company's advance halted for only a few minutes, the Germans (at least I hope it was the Germans) started shelling our area. We were on the side of a steep hill where there was an outcropping of rock with a cavity underneath. It did not take a really smart person to know the safest spot would be close under the rock at the back. Here the chain of command was well demonstrated as the Captain took the choice spot, then the First Sergeant, others of lesser rank, then I, the lowest on the pyramid of army personnel. Because of my less than desirable place of safety, the lower part of my body remained exposed to the falling shells but luckily none came close enough to harm me. Had I been wounded in the most prominently exposed part of my body, it would have been impossible to apply a tourniquet or show my scar in mixed company.

The best foxhole that I ever encountered was not one of my design or digging. By deduction I determined it was dug by a German soldier as a defensive position foxhole. It was beautiful, as far as foxholes go, being narrow, deep and with straight sides with the dirt dispersed so as to not give its location away. It was just deep enough to allow my head and shoulders to rise above the ground level and provided a good view to the approaches. As the shells started to fall I found this foxhole quickly and was thankful to the German soldier who took such care in its fabrication.

The terrain was not as mountainous as the Rockies in the United States, but it did prevent the use of tanks, thus leaving the fighting up to the foot soldier, one of which was myself. It was hard work as the slopes required a lot of effort. I can remember looking down on a small village in a valley and watching an American fighter strafe a target. I do not believe the town was Raon L'Etape, but could have possibly been St. Blaise, France. There were few roads, the few being in the valleys. The area was beautiful with the pine forests. One night it snowed, large flakes of wet snow, and we had to knock the snow off the top of our shelter halves in our foxhole. The trees, with their branches bent under the heavy snow, were beautiful.

One day, as we moved into an area, we received quite a bit of small arms fire from our front with the rounds making noises as they passed by the trees whose tops had been completely removed by artillery fire earlier, ours or theirs. This phenomenon of the sounds of the rifle rounds passing through the trees not too far overhead was interesting. In training in the States we had crawled through a combat obstacle course with live machine gun fire only a foot or two above our bodies, but we had never been exposed to the sound of the rounds passing each tree.

We had to learn as we went as there is no way to exactly duplicate actual combat in training. We had to learn the hard way. We were facing a German army which had been in warfare since 1939, but our experience was limited to about thirty days.

The Sergeant called for a few volunteers to seek out the source of this rifle fire, several men responded, moved out and soon the rifle shots ceased.

At another spot, at another time, we had just undergone a rather strong artillery barrage and afterwards I helped one of our men off the ground as he was shook up. We found that a piece of shrapnel had pierced his canteen which he carried on his hip. Otherwise, he was unharmed—just shook up. I shook his canteen and the piece of shrapnel rattled around inside, thus bringing to a close its role of holding water.

I kept looking for one of the little carbines which could replace my much heavier M1 rifle. I did locate one on the ground, having been discarded, but the reason for its being thrown away was apparent as there was a crease across the barrel undoubtedly caused by a piece of red-hot flying shrapnel.

November 21, 1944, was a red letter day for me. The day had been rather uneventful as far as shelling, small arms fire and other action. We could hear the whispering of the American artillery shells as they passed over our area to hopefully silence the German's large guns. We had stopped for the night, set up our perimeter, dug in and most of the company

A French POW in Stalag VIIA enlarged a wallet photo of my sister, Ellen, who was fourteen at that time. The fee for this art work was paid in cigarettes, the number of which has been forgotten. The finished 5 X 7 pastel is signed Pierre 45, Stalag VIIA. The original wallet photograph is shown in the lower left corner above.

Top: The Expert Infantry Badge
Middle: The Combat Infantry Badge
Bottom: The Bronze Star

The Lindsey family in 1936 posing in front of Texas' most famous landmark, the Alamo in San Antonio. Left to right: Adam Lynn Lindsey (Dad), Adrian L. (Bud) Lindsey, Betty Lindsey, Dorothy Jean Lindsey and in front, Mary Ellen Lindsey. Missing is Mother, Esther Irene, who is the photographer, snapping the picture about 100 years after Davy Crockett, Stephen F. Austin and other Texans unsuccessfully defended the Alamo against Santa Anna and the Mexican Army.

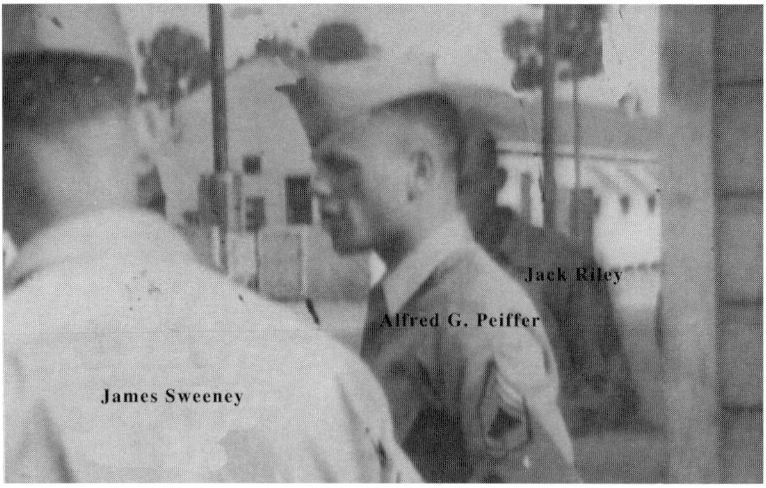

Above: The cadre of the 397th Regimental Headquarters I & R Platoonat Ft. Bragg, North Carolina in 1944. James Sweeney, Alfred G. Peiffer and Jack Riley.

Below: The cadre at Camp Plauche, Louisiana, near New Orleans in 1945. The author, A.L. (Bud) Lindsey is standing, second from left.

Above: Liberated Stalag VIIA POWs on April 29, 1945. The G.I. in the overcoat is Mathis and standing to the right is Garrison. Both POWs were in the 99th Division and were from Dick Cade's outfit. They had been captured earlier. The others are unidentified British POWs. (Photo courtesy of Dick Cade)
Below: Recently liberated POWs at Stalag VIIA walk around the camp area. (Photo courtesy of Dick Cade)

Above: April 29, 1945. An unidentified American Air Force officer utilizes one of the small handcrafted stoves at Stalag VIIA in Germany at Moosburg, near Munich. The camp was liberated about noon on that Sunday morning. These small stoves were fabricated by one or more of the prisoners of war out of cans received in the Red Cross parcels and sold to other POWs for cigarettes, the camp's currency. They consisted of a fire box connected to a blower which could be turned by hand producing high heat with only a minimum of fuel...pieces of cardboard, wood or coal. One of the stoves can bee seen in the foreground. (Photo courtesy of Dick Cade)

After we were liberated from Stalag VIIA on April 19, 1945, I picked up these "souvenirs" from a residence in Moosburg. I have tried to find the owner to return the photos to no avail.

Moosburg, Germany, the site of Stalag VIIA, is located about 25 miles northeast of Munich. It is noted for its church with twin spires. The town suffered little damage during WWII. This picture post card was taken from a residence in Moosburg on April 29, 1945.

broke out "C" rations for a cold bite. I went around the company perimeter collecting the daily report to take back to the company's command post. Since the perimeter was in a semi-circle, I decided to take a short cut across rather than follow the line around, a wrong decision as it turned out.

It was not dark but in the mountains, even though the sun had not set, it was getting dark. Somehow, when I cut across the perimeter, I erroneously bypassed our line, walking between two foxholes. I traveled through the trees slowly realizing that I should have intersected our line, but as I was so sure I was correct I decided to go a little further. I saw a dead German propped up against a pine tree, obviously a victim of that day. This should have alerted me of the fact I was too far out, but since I had only gone about 100 yards, I was not concerned. "Just a wee bit further," I thought. The need-to-know information would have been valuable at this time as no one told me that the German line was "just over the hill, over yonder."

It was very quiet. The only sounds I heard were some distant artillery, not unlike the sounds of a summer thunderstorm in Central Texas. Then there was a brief burst of automatic fire and a single shot, all some distance from my location. The area was free of any underbrush and on a gentle slope high on the mountain. There were large pine or fir trees and visibility was fair.

I was not not particularly being careful as I expected to run into our perimeter very soon. I glanced to my right, perhaps as a result of a movement in the corner of my eye. There were four helmets sticking out a fox hole about twenty yards to my right. For a brief moment I thought I had found Company E's line, but then I noticed that in addition to the four helmets there were four rifles pointed at my mid-section. It was then I realized the helmets were of the German style and I had stumbled into the German's line. They were well dug in in what I would guess was a forward outpost. They saw me before I saw them and, as a western gunfighter would observe, "..they had the drop on me."

I froze. I had several options, none desirable. I could have brought my M1 to bear and perhaps got off a round before they killed me. Another option would have been to turn, run, hit the dirt, roll and otherwise take evasive action. Another option, which didn't occur to me until much later, would have been to ask the quartet of German soldiers to surrender to me. This would not have been likely, but I should have tried.

So much for my quick thinking.

With four of them and only one of me, it would have been likely I would have been killed. The best option, I decided, was to surrender. All of this only took a few seconds as I could see that the four Germans, at a distance of only about twenty yards, clearly had the upper hand. I felt pretty foolish walking up on the German outpost, allowing them to spot me before I spotted them. So much for my attendance at scouting school.

I raised my hands and arms above my head, a universal sign of surrender. One of the quartet asked a single word question, "Kamerad?" a universal verbal question of surrender.

I answered, "Comrade."

<u>WESTERN UNION TELEGRAM</u>

DC 32 43 GOVT=WUX WASHINGTON DC DEC 6 155P

MRS ESTHER I LINDSEY

1103 SOUTH CHINA ST

THE SECRETARY OF WAR DESIRES ME TO EXPRESS HIS DEEP REGRET THAT YOUR SON PRIVATE ADRIAN L. LINDSEY HAS BEEN REPORTED MISSING IN ACTION SINCE TWENTY ONE NOVEMBER IN FRANCE IF FURTHER DETAILS OR OTHER INFORMATION ARE RECEIVED YOU WILL BE PROMPTLY NOTIFIED=

DUNLOP ACTING THE ADJUTANT GENERAL

CHAPTER SIX

KRIEGIE

STALAG VIIA
MOOSBURG, GERMANY

One of the German soldiers disarmed me, taking my M1 and grenades, then he marched me a short distance down the mountain to a central operation point which I would guess would be similar to our regimental command post. As we moved into their area I took note of the German's facilities, such as gun positions and other equipment. I noted that they had wagons and mobile equipment drawn by horses rather than gasoline powered vehicles. They took me to a building, into a room which was occupied by several German soldiers who indicated that I should sit on the floor. This I did, using my helmet as a seat.

After a time—it was almost dark by now—the Germans indicated I should accompany a young soldier out of the building. This soldier was very young, perhaps younger than I, and seemed very nervous about having the responsibility of guarding me all alone. He told me, by sign language, that I should precede him down the middle of the road. We had only gone about 100 feet when he said "Halt," or something to that effect. I stopped and turned, facing him from about 15 feet. He had his rifle trained on me and I thought perhaps he had been ordered to shoot me, but that was not the case. He indicated, again by sign language, that he wished for me to give him my watch. I took off my watch and tossed it to him. This was not a great loss, probably an Elgin which kept only approximate time.

The trip from the Vosges Mountains to the POW camp at Moosburg, near Munich, a distance of over 200 miles, took several days to two weeks, the exact time or route I do not remember. We walked and rode civilian trains, but mostly walked, always under guard. As I moved further east I was joined by other prisoners who had been captured in other areas and from other outfits.

At one location, and I believe it was still in France, in the Rhine River valley, I was interrogated by two German officers. The building was a two story building of masonry construction overlooking a road which was lined with trees and a valley with open fields and a brook. Under other circumstances I would have enjoyed the view. The two German officers interrogated me one after the other using what I learned later to be the "good guy, bad guy" technique. The bad guy threatened to have me shot if I did not tell him everything he wanted to know. The good guy tried to draw me into a friendly conversation that he might extract vital information, information which was nonexistent in my person. I revealed little and it did not take the two interviewers long to realize I knew less about the Allied operations than anyone they had run into during the entire war up to that time. I feel sure my appearance did contribute somewhat to their decision to stop the interrogation as it was unlikely I could help their side. I must have looked like a character out of Bill Mauldin's comic strip...a sad sack. The bad guy did not have me shot, and the good guy wished me good luck saying, "For you the war is over," an expression which I heard more than once. An expression which was not exactly accurate.

The information that might be gleaned from the interrogations of the captured army privates such as myself could be useful in finding the movement and make-up of a new group of troops such as the 100th Infantry Division. We naturally had all reference to our outfit removed along with any papers which we might carry. I learned later, many years after the war, Axis Sally, on her daily German radio broadcast had welcomed our division to Marseilles as we landed.

The Air Corps crews who were shot down over Germany and German territory, were subjected to much more intense interrogation, as the men who flew the fighters or were crews on the B-17s did know information which the Germans sought.

At one town we disembarked from a civilian train, a group of perhaps ten POW's with four guards, and were greeted by an angry group of civilians who wished to do us bodily harm. They were prevented from doing so by the guards. I would guess their town had been subjected to a massive bombing the night or day before, perhaps with misdirected bombs.

Earlier, when we were fewer in number, perhaps five with two guards, we were being marched down a country road when we heard an American fighter plane. It was easy to identify the sounds of a German fighter and an American plane as the German aircraft motors made an irregular sound while the American plane has an even sound. The guards urged us to run into a building located only fifty yards or so up the road. We could hear the American plane as it started a strafing run on our group. We made it to the entrance to the building and turned left down the hallway into a room. The fighter strafed the entrance to the building with some of the rounds ricocheting down the hallway, creating sparks. I don't know what type of fighter this was, nor do I have any idea why the pilot decided to fire on a small group of men of which only two were armed, and five were American POWs. I feel sure it was hard to identify with accuracy such a group from the air. Perhaps it had been a dull day for him and a target such as our group was the best he had. It would be interesting to run into this pilot one day and listen to his story. Better yet, I would like to view the 16mm film from his gun camera had he filmed the entire episode, which I doubt.

We spent at least two nights in a large building surrounded by a high stone fence. This building may have been utilized as a barn at one time. The Germans had a large group of French POWs in one end of the barn and a similar group of American POWs in the other end, each being prohibited from mixing. Our outdoor latrine was the familiar open pit with a structure of logs placed above. There was one log to sit on and one on which to rest your back and prevent you from falling into the pit. I, as did most of the group, suffered from “the G.I.s”, a condition that I would nurse for about thirty days, caused by the abrupt change of diet and the water. It was very cold and the “sitting” log was covered with frost which I encountered several times each night during our tenure at this location. I tried to time my trips so the “sitting” log was still warm from the previous user. There was danger of sticking to the frost-covered log during the intense cold.

Near the Rhine river we were placed in a large building equipped with cells, evidently a regular jail or prison which was apparently vacated except for the in-transit POWs.

Eventually we reached Stalag VIIA at Moosburg, Germany, a distance of about 225 miles, as the crow flies, from where I was captured in France. Moosburg is a small town in Southern Germany about

25 miles northeast of Munich. At Stalag VIIA, we were interviewed, for what purpose I do not know, and given German POW dog tags. I told the interviewer I had been a soda jerk in civilian life. I had to explain exactly what type of work was involved by being a soda jerk. I suspected the POW camp did not have a soda fountain, a suspicion that certainly proved to be true. I was assigned to barracks fifty-three, the beginning of five months of hunger.

Stalag VIIA, one of many in Germany, was built in 1939 and was designed for about 10,000 men, on about 85 acres. The large majority of the prisoners were French (about 38,000), with about 8,000 British, almost 6,000 American, 14,000 Russian and soldiers from other countries to total almost 80,000 at the time of its liberation in late April of 1945.

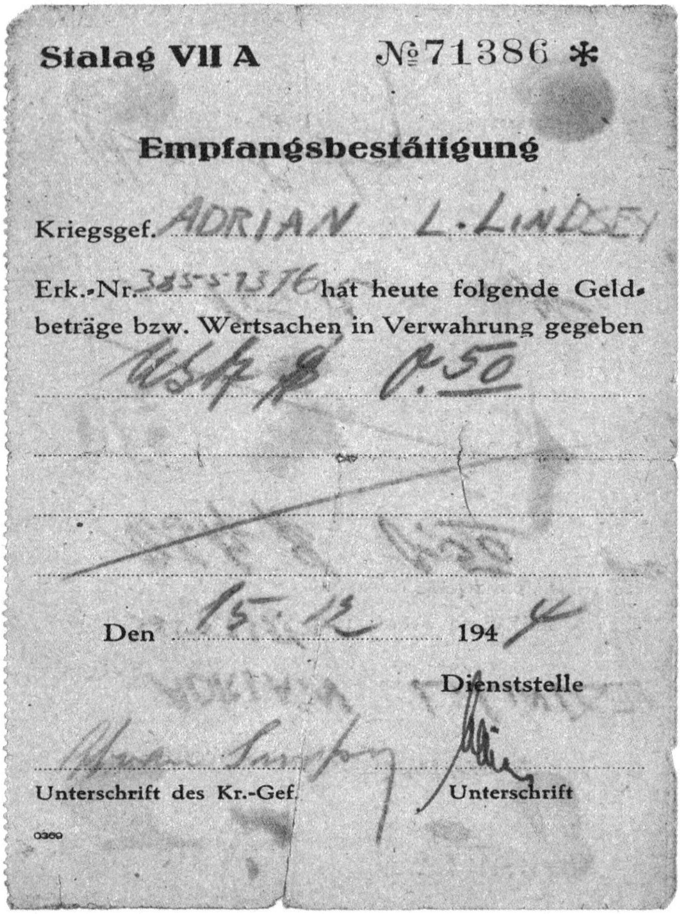

Stalag VII A №71386 *

Empfangsbestätigung

Kriegsgef. ADRIAN L. LINDSEY

Erk.-Nr. 38559376 hat heute folgende Geld- beträge bzw. Wertsachen in Verwahrung gegeben

USA $ 0.50

Den 15-12 1944

Dienststelle

Unterschrift des Kr.-Gef. Unterschrift

0369

I was given a receipt for any money which I had. The rough translation is "Acknowledgment of receipt. 38559376 has today following cash." The receipt has the signature of the prisoner (myself) and the signature of the German officer. I had fifty cents in my pockets. It is dated 15-12-44, the European dating differing from the American way, showing the day before the month. Thus, the date was December 15, 1944

Letter from Stalag VIIA, Moosburg, Germany, Dec 31, 1944. *(The stationery was a standard form issued by the Germans to the prisoners to write letters. I do not know when this letter was received in Brady. Even though I wrote as many letters as allowed during the six months as a captive, this is the only one received in Brady. I received no mail while in Stalag VIIA.)*

Dearest Mom,

Lady, I've been doing a lot of thinking since I left the States. I wanted to write and tell you a lot of things before I was captured but didn't get a chance. The most important thing that I wanted to tell you was how much I appreciated having a sweet gal like you for a mother. I don't mind admitting that I get homesick a lot--but I'm alive and well. For gosh's sake don't worry about this guy, he'll get along OK. It's not such a bad existence--I've made some very good buddies. Xmas wasn't like being home by a long shot--had a Red Cross parcel--good American food. Here's hoping that '45 is a better year for everybody---all my love, Bud

We called ourselves "Kriegies" which was short for the German "Kriegsgefangener," translation of which would be "prisoner of war," a name which somehow seemed to fit our appearance.

The clothes we wore were the ones we wore when captured and had not changed, except for our socks, since we went on line in France. I had not taken a bath since we left Marseilles, some thirty days before.

It was cold, winter time, and my fellow prisoners were just as "gamy" as I. Later during my imprisonment I would be able to enjoy two hot-water showers of a few minutes duration during the five months as a POW. The two showers offered only a short relief from the body lice and other parasites for which we acted as hosts. After the infrequent shower we put the same clothes back on our momentarily clean torsos, where the wee creatures marched, goose stepping, back in place. However, the Germans did shave our pubic hair, spray our private parts areas with some type of dust thus perhaps inhibiting the parasites.

I was lucky in one sense to be a prisoner at Stalag VIIA, a facility which eventually overflowed with about eighty thousand American, French, British, British subjects, Russians and Canadians and was considered to be the better of the many POW camps scattered across Germany. Which was not saying a lot as conditions were primitive at the best. We were housed in permanent wooden barracks with a single coal-fired stove for heating, for which we had no coal.

The facilities were fairly well duplicated in the movie, Stalag 17, starring William Holden released in 1953. In the movie the barracks may have housed thirty POWs, however one report stated the barracks in Moosburg were designed for ten men. In real life at barracks fifty-three in Stalag VIIA we numbered over one hundred. One noticeable difference between the movie and real life in Stalag VIIA was in the cleanliness of the inmates. William Holden and the other members of the cast of Stalag17 could go home after the day's "take" and enjoy good food and a hot bath, not so at Stalag VIIA. We were very dirty —— and hungry. The actors in the movie appeared to be well fed, again not so in Stalag VIIA.

We had a single water faucet located outside which was turned on only during certain daylight hours. There was always a line at the faucet waiting to suck out the water when the pump was idle. The person sucking on the hydrant would place his thumb in the opening until the next person in line was in position to suck, an activity which would give a member of the Department of Health a fit of apoplexy. Actually just about everything which happened in Stalag VIIA would have the same effect on a Department of Health employee. Sanitary conditions were minimal with not enough water to wash our hands or eating utensils, such as they were, consequently diarrhea was a constant problem.

Our latrine facilities were not in the open, but were covered, and consisted of an open pit with perhaps six stations not unlike the primitive outhouses of rural Texas in the thirties. One report which I read after the war indicated the Germans had issued rolls of toilet paper: however, it must have been earlier in the war as I saw none in Stalag VIIA. You made out with what you could scrounge from the Red Cross parcels or other sources, or did without. The open pit cess pool was sucked out only when in danger of overflowing by a vehicle which we dubbed "The Honey Wagon." I was told the honey wagon then utilized its contents as fertilizer for farming, a common practice in Europe, I understood.

Stalag VIIA , not unlike the other POW camps in Germany, was constructed of wooden barracks surrounded by a double fence of barbed wire, the two fences being separated by about six feet, with coiled wire between the two fences. Inside the perimeter of the double-fence was the so called trip wire, a single strand of wire mounted only two feet or less above the ground on stakes, and located perhaps twenty feet inside the double wired perimeter fence. It was forbidden to go past the trip wire as doing so was to invite being shot by one of the guards in the several guard towers located around the perimeter of the camp.

Each of the barracks was surrounded by a single layered barbed wire fence, separating each barracks from the next. The gates of these barrack's fences were closed after dark. Naturally the entire camp area was swept by searchlights which were mounted and manned in the guard towers. It was forbidden to trade between the wired enclosures after dark. Though I did not witness nor hear the shooting, it was rumored that one of the American POWs was shot as he traded across the fence surrounding his barracks after dark.

The German military generally stayed within the guide lines which were agreed upon at an earlier meeting many years prior to WWII in Geneva, Switzerland, which dealt with the treatment of prisoners of war. Germany, Britain and the United States signed the agreement. Russia and Japan did not. One of the articles agreed upon was that privates would be required to work in non-war related jobs. Another important agreement was that the signed parties would provide the prisoners with the same quality of food which was supplied to the retaining country's army; that is, the Americans who were prisoners of the Germans would receive the same rations as the German soldiers.

Also, the signers of the agreement would receive Red Cross parcels, thus the Russian prisoners did not receive the much needed food provided by these parcels.

Another part of the Geneva agreement dealt with

payment to the POWs who were recruited for non-military type of work by the detaining countries. It was agreed that the workers be paid for their work. I read one report many years later which stated this figure was $13 per month, working six days a week. Pay was not mentioned by the Germans at Stalag VIIA; however, the American POWs, including myself, did receive payment much later, after we had returned to the States, for our working during our time as prisoners of war, the amount of which I do not remember. It was not much and some might say we were overpaid.

The nationalities were separated into different compounds within Stalag VIIA with the officers being separated from the enlisted men, hardly any different from the American Army criteria. The enlisted men's barracks were overseen by British non-commissioned officers, such as our equivalent of Buck Sergeants and Corporals. Our barracks, number fifty-three, had, I believe, three British non-commissioned officers who were supposed to maintain a semblance of order. They had a small room at one end of the barracks, a deluxe accommodation by our standards. These non-commissioned British officers in our barracks were not well liked by our group. Their demeanor was aloof, conceited and gave the impression they considered the American G.I.s to be inferior, an attitude which did not set well with our group, especially a Texan, the best soda-jerk in Central Texas.

During the time just prior to Christmas of 1944, we were able to observe the German civilians in Munich having Christmas decorations, however limited in quantity, not unlike those displayed in my hometown. This was somewhat a surprise to us as we thought the German civilians were not allowed to exhibit signs of Christianity.

Most of us began to get the Christmas spirit and tempered our negative feelings of the British noncom cadre at Barracks 53. I don't remember who in our barracks originated the thought but we took up a collection of cigarettes to give the British cadre as a Christmas gift. The number of cigarettes was substantial and, by standards of a POW in Stalag VIIA, they became wealthy. We did not expect a gift, or gifts, in return as it would have been impractical, if not impossible, for the British cadre to supply such. I suppose The Brits did thank us, but they still looked upon us as being ill-bred and uncouth. And we still looked upon them as being "uppity."

The diet of the dark, heavy German bread created quite a bit of intestinal gas which had to be emitted on occasion in public places. This was a real problem for me, while in transit from the place of my capture and the prison camp at Moosburg, as we were riding a civilian train for some hours one night and I, along with other prisoners, had no choice but to get rid of the gas. We tried to look innocent and hoped the others on the train would blame the German guards. However, we did refrain from any finger pointing.

The gas problem persisted while in Stalag VIIA and became the sport of some of the men in barracks 53. At the time one of the men had the "urge" he would jump up on the single table in the barracks, position himself so that his posterior was handy and yell, "Match." Anyone who might have an extra match and wished to use it for the purpose could ignite the expelled body gasses, an activity which might be viewed by the British cadre and others as being a sign of poor upbringing.

Most of the men in our barracks were from the northern states and being the only one from Texas, naturally I was called "Tex." We were in groups of twelve, being assigned to bunks in a tier of that same number. We were given a single German blanket and slept on (or in) the three story high bunk bends which were about a foot too short and six inches too narrow. The bunks were equipped with a thin mattress of burlap type material and stuffed with straw, and infested with every type of parasite known to man, dogs, chickens and other and livestock.

The soldiers having the rank of private, I being

one, were lucky in one respect—we had a free ride into Munich. True, we were supposed to work shoveling snow and debris, but we became masters of shovel-leaning, a working technique not unrecognized by the guards, but some did not care. Working in Munich allowed the POWs to trade any articles or foodstuff items from the Red Cross parcels for food, namely the heavy, dark German loaves of bread. A normal sized loaf of this bread may have weighed five pounds—it was very dense, but filling. Filling was what we needed. I feel that the nutritional benefits of this German bread were not great—some said it consisted mostly of sawdust—but it was the best we had.

The Red Cross parcels were wonderful and gave us the calories that were lacking in the daily food the Germans furnished. Most of us used the cigarettes that came in the parcels for trading both in Munich and within the camp. Most of us smoked, but had not acquired the habit to such a degree we could not forsake such. Cigarettes were our monetary system, a pack of Chesterfields buying as much as three loaves of German dark bread.

The brands of cigarettes the parcels usually contained were either Old Gold or Chesterfield brands, the least desirable of the American brands. Most G.I.s felt the Lucky Strikes went to the officers. None were ever found in the Red Cross parcels. The British Red Cross parcels contained a lot of mutton and other strange items along with Players cigarettes, the least desirable of all cigarettes. Never the less, any brand of American or British cigarettes were relished by the German civilians and the German guards.

The number of loaves of German bread which might be traded for a package of American cigarettes varied with the supply and demand. When I first became involved in trading cigarettes for bread, a package of twenty cigarettes would trade for perhaps four loaves, but with the influx of more prisoners after the battle of he bulge, this figure dropped to two or three loaves.

Naturally it was "verboten" (forbidden) to trade with the German civilians, but by bribing the German guards, it was allowed to some extent. The trades with the German civilians would be hurried with the guards being sure there were no unwanted observers of the activity. I should imagine the American and British POWs were the source of the major part of the black market in Germany.

Periodically the POWs were searched at the main gate as we entered upon returning from work parties. This was a quick search with only about one in five or six being stopped for a "patting" down. If bread was found it was removed from the POW and tossed into a growing pile on the ground. I had found a French overcoat for which I traded. The reason I desired this type of coat was because it flared at the bottom and I was able to sew two pockets on the bottom inside of the coat to be used to place loaves of bread, a location that would not be noticed in the cursory search at the gate. Another technique quickly adopted by the POWs was to jockey into position at the gate where the chances of being the one in six searched would be unlikely. My overcoat idea worked quite well and I was never relieved of bread which was in the pockets.

One night after dark, when we were being searched under searchlights, I observed a POW in front of me with his hands raised above his head being searched for bread with the guard patting him down. But the clever POW had a loaf of German bread in each of his hands which were raised above the guard's notice. He passed in the gate with his bread being intact.

Our normal day started before daylight, the exact time could not be noted by myself as the young German guard had requested my Elgin back in the Vosges Mountains in France. But, we did not need watches as the Germans set our schedules and knowing the time was unnecessary. We were roused before daylight, filed out of the barracks and stood in ranks for "rappel" (roll call). If we were slow exiting the barracks, the Germans would send in a guard dog to hasten the process. Naturally these dogs were German Shepherds. After the roll call we would have a short time to go to the latrine. We received a cup of a hot drink which the Germans called coffee, bearing no resemblance to Folger's, Maxwell House or Early Bird brands. One report stated that the ersatz coffee was made from oak leaves and coal. The best you could say of it was it was hot. That was breakfast.

We would then be ready to be called out to march to the railway depot in Moosburg, only a short distance from the camp. We would be loaded into the famous 40 and 8 European boxcars for the trip to Munich. These box cars were designed to hold forty men or eight horses, hence the name 40 and 8. The Germans must have called them "100 and 8" as they would crowd about 100 of us in each car. As the weather was very cold it was beneficial that we were so crowded in order to share each other's body heat and perhaps a parasite or two.

Weather permitting, we slid the large doors of the boxcars open so we could have some air circulation and see the countryside. The short distance between Moosburg and the railroad terminal at Munich was pretty, with woods, fields and some small streams.

We even could see deer grazing in some of the fields, which were viewed by us a potential meal rather than as a part of the scenery.

Most of the German guards were older — perhaps veterans of WWI — some being in their forties. Some may have been wounded previously and the guard duty at Stalag VIIA would have been considered as easy duty. None could speak English and none of our group could speak German, except for a very few words, so we and they utilized signs and body language to communicate. Ted Doty, one of the men in our tier of bunks, recently reminded me of a guard whom we called "Charlie." Charlie was one of the older guards and was a good sort. We were lucky when we drew Charlie as one of the two guards who drew the duty of guarding a group of ten POWs while working Munich as Charlie, and other guards of his temperament, would allow the POWs to trade with civilian women which was verboten. We recalled one cold morning as we boarded the boxcars in Moosburg and the guard Charlie was designated to be in our box car. The boxcars were rather high off the ground and it was a giant step to get into the opening. Charlie had some trouble getting in so he handed his rifle to one of us, we helped him in and politely handed back his rifle. I've often wondered if Charlie—we never knew his real name—survived the war and, if so, how he spent his life.

<u>WESTERN UNION TELEGRAM</u>

DJ119 33 GOVT=WUX WASHINGTON DC MAR 9 355P

MRS ESTHER I LINDSEY

1103 SOUTH CHINA ST BRADY TEX=

REPORT JUST RECEIVED THROUGH THE INTERNATIONAL RED CROSS STATES THAT YOUR SON PRIVATE ADRIAN L LINDSEY IS A PRISONER OF WAR OF THE GERMAN GOVERNMENT LETTER OF INFORMATION FOLLOWS FROM PROVOST MARSHAL GENERAL=

ULIO THE ADJUTANT GENERAL.

It is interesting to me that the telegram advising my family of the fact I was a POW was dated March 9, 1945, more than three months after my capture in Southeastern France. I have no idea as to the delivery date of the single letter home from Stalag VIIA, written in late December of 1944.

We worked most days in Munich with the days off being on Sunday and when the trains could not run because of the damage caused by the air raids of the previous day or night by the British and American Air Forces. It was very evident the war was being won by our side, the good guys, as at night we could see and hear the raids by the British RAF on the rail yards in Munich and Augsburg. Some days there would be a steady stream of contrails from B-17s visible in the sky.

The only German aircraft we observed in the sky over Moosburg was one of the early jet fighters, one of the few which the Germans manufactured. The pilot would fly, more than on one occasion, at a low altitude near Stalag VIIA and disappear in the distance with a roar. Of course, we did not know, other than the object being an aircraft, what in the Sam Hill was that.

One of the men in our barracks had a small Bible which he shared with everyone. Many of us, including myself, took advantage of his offer and read the Bible from cover to cover. Church services were offered aboard ship on the journey from the States to France, but little time was available for such after we landed in France. Earlier in the war it was my understanding church services were held at Stalag VIIA; however, I was not aware of any being held after I arrived in early December of 1944. I believe if someone had wished to conduct religious service the camp's Commandant, Obverst Burger, would not have interfered.

It would be rare indeed to find a soldier of either side who had not acquired a type of "fox hole" religion during a time when artillery rounds were falling nearby, many making adamant promises to God, some kept and some not kept after the shelling ceased and the war was over.

The food served at Stalag VIIA was only minimal. I have no idea how many calories were involved. There were certainly no calories in the cup of hot so-called coffee we had each morning. Lunch was usually a cup of barley, rutabaga or cabbage soup. Our evening meal was a tad better being soup and occasional piece of meat, of unknown origin, and a chunk of the dark German bread, and sometimes potatoes, boiled with their skins intact.

For the evening distribution of the barley, rutabaga or cabbage soup, each twelve-man group would alternate in spooning out the portions out of a large kettle which appeared to hold 20 or so gallons. The privilege of dispensing the soup was alternated between the groups each day. One evening as our group's turn came to "cater" the evening's soup pot, I was selected to be the dispenser. Using a large ladle, I carefully gave each POW a ladle full in their cups. Unfortunately I ran out of soup with about six or eight men being left without soup. I being one of the six or eight who went to bed hungry, not an unusual circumstance. There was naturally some grumbling and negative comments tossed my way, criticizing my ability as a soup dispenser, but no outward threats upon my life.

One day I traded cigarettes for what the POW vender called a rabbit, already skinned, dressed and ready for cooking. I was able to cook the dressed animal on the little blower type cook stove. I'm not sure now, or then, if it was indeed a rabbit. It could have been a cat or other small animal including a very large rat. It was delicious!

Our Red Cross parcels were available depending on transportation by the Germans and the temperament of the German command. We were in groups of twelve, which coincided with our bunk tiers, to receive the parcels. Depending on the availability, sometimes we had four men on a parcel per week, sometimes two, sometimes none, but at Christmas of 1944, we received a parcel per POW.

We welcomed any parcel, but the American parcels were most desired over the British as they contained coffee, rather than tea; American cigarettes; cheese, rather than plum pudding; crackers; sugar cubes; powdered milk; Spam rather than mutton. Hormel, the inventor of Spam, may have won the war, of course with a little help from General Eisenhower and myself.

We found we could crumble the German bread, mix it with some powdered milk, add sugar, raisins, put the mixture in an empty can and hang it out the window to freeze—it made a nice pudding or whatever you might call it.

One report calculated the calories obtained from the German rations of soup and bread would be about 800 per day. Even the Russians who were supposedly fed twice the German ration would only receive about 1600 per day, a figure which I understand is minimal for an adult under such conditions.

The typical American Red Cross parcel consisted

of four ounces of powdered coffee, twelve ounces of corned beef or Spam, eight ounces of sugar cubes, sixteen ounces of powdered milk, eight ounces of crackers, four ounces of orange concentrate, eight ounces of cheese, a small bar of soap, a chocolate bar and some raisins or prunes. There were also packages of cigarettes. Each parcel was designed for one parcel per man per week, a goal hardly ever reached. The typical distribution was one parcel per week for four men, or perhaps up to twelve men.

One report which I read estimated the calorie content of a Red Cross parcel was about 7,000 calories.

Some Red Cross parcels of clothing, toilet paper and other necessities were distributed to other camps, however, I was never the recipient of any or had knowledge of any in Stalag VIIA.

Any place, other than at Stalag VIIA, when you have a group of nineteen year old Army soldiers together, the talk naturally turns to girls and their physical merits, with some of the less gentlemanly conversationalists telling all of their exploits with the opposite sex. Even though being young men with high testosterone levels, girls were mentioned but the main subject of conversation was food. Home cooking and what our mothers cooked. We were constantly hungry and the conversations about food were not welcomed by all as talking about food was mental torture to some. There was one POW who bunked in the tier next to mine, on the top bunk (I have forgotten his name) who withdrew, did not communicate with the others and did not stand up to life in POW camp very well. I offered the group the benefit of my knowledge of how to mix up delicious malts or milk shakes of various flavors, ice cream sodas, coke floats — we called them frosted cokes — and the best hamburgers in Central Texas. I feel sure the withdrawn POW on the top bunk next to ours did not appreciate my narration.

During our captivity we did not discuss the events leading up to our capture and our ordeals from that time until we arrived at Stalag VIIA. Always our conversations centered on other subjects other than the war.

Each of us had plans of what to do when, and if, we got back home and what type of vocation we would seek. I had some experience in drug store pharmacy work, mixing cough syrups and the like, and thought I would like to become a pharmacist before I was imprisoned by the Germans. After my capture, and experiencing such hunger pains, I thought I would like to open a bakery.

There was very little stealing between the POWs and one of us could put his hoarded food and other belongings at his bunk and be reasonably certain it would still be there after returning from a work detail in Munich.

When we were not working in Munich we could, weather permitting, go to the parade ground and walk the perimeter, staying carefully away from the trip wire.

The camp had an open air stage where some innovative prisoners sometimes performed, showing their talents, desiring cigarettes rather than applause for their efforts. A black soldier, one of the few, if not the only one in camp, was very talented doing a tap dance, not unlike Sammy Davis, Jr. I was told this soldier was captured after his ship was sunk not far off the North Carolina coast two days after the war with Germany was declared. I have no idea if the story is true, as I never asked the question of the tap dancer.

One of the men in our group was very adept at acting out and singing the complete tune, "Juke Box Saturday Night," which was quite popular at the time. One of the men had a deck of cards and I learned to play pinochle, a card game which was new to me.

Nothing was wasted. Paper was at a premium. We had no toilet paper and even though my dysentery had somehow cured itself, many of the men had digestive problems. The empty cans obtained from the Red Cross parcels were utilized for cooking and saved as they had value in trading.

There were a few who were skillful with their hands and had somehow obtained some tools to fashion the cans into small stoves which had a blower to force air into the fire box, not unlike a blacksmith's forge. These small stoves were available from the stove entrepreneurs for cigarettes. Late on a still evening you could see the entire parade ground in the middle of the camp spotted with POWs kneeling, turning the blower wheel on the little stoves, heating up something to eat.

One day while we were working in Munich a young boy of about 10 years of age rode by our group of ten POWs and stopped. His English was passable and, with the permission of the two German guards, visited with us at length. He identified himself as Ludwig Herman B. Reischboeck. We introduced ourselves, Albert Delano, Rudolph Shafer and myself. We conversed at length and gave the young man our home addresses in the States and showed him pictures of our families. The young boy offered to see if he could find toothbrushes for us and we agreed to give him cigarettes for the same. Unfortunately the guards moved us to go back to Moosburg or to an air raid shelter, a common daily occurrence, before the young lad returned, so we spent the duration of our confinement having to brush our teeth with water and our fingers.

It was not uncommon to spend a portion of each day we were in Munich in an air raid shelter. The American Air Force would bomb the railroads and other targets in or near Munich almost daily. When the alarm was sounded, the guards would herd the POWs into the nearest air raid shelter where we waited, with the civilians, for the all clear to sound.

At another time, while working in Munich, a young girl walked by our group. This resulted in all of us, including the two guards, watching her approach and her departure. As she walked past our group one of the POWs remarked, in English, something to the effect that he would like to know her better — nothing vulgar or out of taste luckily as she turned and came back engaging us in conversation in perfect English.

There was a Frenchman in camp who offered to paint pictures for cigarettes. His speciality was to copy and enlarge a photograph. I had somehow retained my wallet, sans money, in which was a small school class picture of my little sister, Mary Ellen. I "commissioned" this artist to enlarge the small photo to about a 5X7 size. I managed to keep the picture and get it back to the States and it now hangs, framed, in a place of prominence in our home. The picture is signed and dated by the artist: "Pierre 45, Stalag VIIA." It is difficult to read the name, but I believe it is "Pierre." I had made notes on the back of the little wallet photo indicating to the French artist the color of Ellen's hair and her eyes. I have no idea where the French artist obtained the paper, water colors and other materials to accomplish his paintings.

Several POWs, barbers in civilian life, set up shop in Stalag VIIA and would cut your hair for a few cigarettes. The quality of their talents of cutting and styling hair were lacking, but we were not interested in the cosmetic quality of our hair dos, but in getting rid of surplus hair, a great place for lice to take up residence. The self appointed barbers certainly did not have to have a barber's license, only a set of shears being the only qualification for the vocation.

Others had other enterprises, one being a crap game with the bets being in cigarettes. I once risked two cigarettes in one of these games to no avail. I decided, prior suspicions confirmed, I was not a gambler. Besides two cigarettes could be traded for a slice of the dark German bread.

It was common for the POWs to carefully open the cellophane outer wrapping of a package of American cigarettes at the bottom of the package and remove the cellophane sleeve from the package. Then the package of twenty cigarettes was opened from the top, four cigarettes removed, the package closed and the cellophane covering placed back on the package. The cellophane sleeve kept the top of the package closed and, unless closely inspected, appeared to be a package of twenty cigarettes which was used to trade to the German civilians for bread. The four loose cigarettes then could be saved to smoke (rarely) or to trade within the camp with other POWs.

Also we would take the tea from the British parcels, enjoy the brewed tea, spread the tea leaves out to dry, place them back in the carefully opened original package and trade the used tea leaves for bread. This worked very well as the German civilians must make a trade quickly as trading with the POWs was forbidden and they could not take the time to carefully inspect their "purchase." Those German civilians who traded for used English tea leaves may have blamed the British on their poor quality and not the American POW who offered the weak leaves in trade. I feel badly that I took part in cheating the German housewives now, but at the time it seemed the thing to do.

The German civilians had a very rough time. They could only live from day to day, not knowing if there would be any food to eat for that day, water to drink or fuel to stay warm. Parts of Munich were almost total rubble, especially near the railway center. I remember seeing the railroad tracks twisted and turned in the air looking like a giant ladder, the ties being the rungs. It was not unusual for us Kriegies to be called out to work, march to the train only to have the trip canceled because of the damage to the rails from the night before.

We were able to pocket a few of the coal "briquettes" which were loose in the railroad yards in Munich to fuel our barracks stove and the small cooking stoves which most of us possessed. We sometimes were able to find paper or wood scraps, paper always being in demand to use as toilet paper. I also would scoop up some gravel, check carefully to see if the guards were watching and drop the gravel into the lubricating boxes on the wheels of the railroad freight cars. I doubt that this shortened the war whatsoever, and there was the danger that I might have been spotted and shot. Being shot on the spot would have been unlikely unless you happened to be spotted by an over zealous guard who would not think of the problem of documenting the event (the German Army was good about such) and getting rid of the body, which would take some time and would disrupt the normal routine. It would be more likely I would have been sent to the "sonder barracks," or the isoliererbracken, where the food would be bread and water with no Red Cross parcels allowed.

It would have been easy to escape. There was no need to dig a tunnel for escape purposes if you were a private. All one of us had to do would be to tell the guard, while we were in Munich, you had to relieve yourself behind a pile of rubble, place your shovel on your shoulder and walk away. But to what? None of us could speak enough German to get by and could not be mistaken, even though we looked the part, for a misplaced person or "hobo." We would have been recaptured and returned to spend a term of time in the sonder barracks back at Stalag VIIA on bread and water. There was not enough civilian sympathy toward an American POW to receive any help in escaping. Also, we all knew, along with the German cadre, the war was winding down and it was only a matter of a short time before the Germans were defeated, most of them seeing the reality of such.

We had not received any Red Cross parcels in a couple of weeks during one period, consequently, I was out of everything to eat except the daily cup of soup, a slice of bread and perhaps a potato. We were in Munich and two little German ladies approached our working group. We had "good" guards that day and they allowed us to trade with the ladies. Unfortunately I had nothing to trade as our cigarettes from the Red Cross parcels were not available. I thought of my high school class ring and showed it to the two ladies. They offered me three loaves of the dark German bread and I quickly accepted.

A pleasant incident happened one day while we were working in Munich. I'm not sure if there was ten of us in the group or not. I don't believe our group was over four in number and I do not know why we were such a small group with a single guard as we usually were in groups of ten with two guards. We had been working for some time when the guard motioned for us to go with him into a cafe which was nearby. We did and he ordered each of us a stein of dark German beer. Naturally, we did not decline. It was perhaps the best beer I had ever tasted. I do not know if it "was on the house" or not, as I do not recall the guard paying for the beer. Certainly we did not have any money to do so.

With such crowded conditions, it was probable there might be an epidemic of some type of disease, such as measles; however, we all had more than enough preventive shots in the army and I heard of no problems other than my contacting mumps late in my confinement. One report which I read some years later indicated the Russian prisoners had some problems with cholera. I, along with many, many others suffered with diarrhea early in my confinement and I developed a raw sore which extended from my anus to my scrotum and persisted for a couple of weeks. With the help of a fellow prisoner, Harold Camp, a medic and fellow prisoner, I was able to clear this up as he somehow obtained some talc.

When the German Army launched the "Battle of the Bulge" in December of 1944, the German guards were elated, as they felt that they were going to win the war. We knew better as it was evident to us the Germans did not have the resources to do so. The late December offensive by the German Army was only a setback. Likewise later, the death of Franklin D. Roosevelt was portrayed as a victory by the German guards. They just did not understand the structure of the American system as the death of F.D.R. had little to do with the progress of the war in Europe against the Germans.

It was hard for me to understand the German's thinking. The few Germans that I had the chance to converse with, they being able to speak English, told me they could not understand why the Americans had any business in getting into the war. I had a long conversation with a German guard on a train somewhere between the Vosges Mountains and Stalag VIIA, a time when we discussed the merits of the United States getting involved. I was unable to change his outlook and he was unable to change mine. We left it at that.

We did not know about the German "death" camps despite the fact that Dachau was located just on the northwest outskirts of Munich. One day we had been working in Munich, shoveling snow and whatever, and had assembled at the rail terminal to get the meager lunch that would be provided. There were about two hundred of us on one end of the raised railway platform and we observed a like number of men, obviously prisoners, assembled about 100 feet away on the other end of the platform. They were a sad looking group, dressed in striped pajama type of convict attire. They were without coats and the day was very cold. We were thin, but the convict group would have certainly won any contest where weight loss was compared. They were pitiful, to say the least. I thought that surely they must be murderers, rapists and other felons of the worst sort.

They also were waiting for the soup which would be their lunch, guarded by German guards with German Shepherd guard dogs (we only saw the guard dogs utilized infrequently to run into the barracks to roust the slow POWs). The German men arrived with a large kettle of soup for the pitiful looking group and sat it down in their end of the platform. Immediately, in unison and silently without any command, the large group rushed the kettle of soup. The guards then turned the two German Shepherd guard dogs loose, who, snarling and snapping, turned on the men in the striped pajama-type clothing. The group's rushing the kettle and their retreat reminded me of a ripened wheat field caught in the wind with the tops all rippling in one direction, then the wind direction changing and the tops bowing in the opposite direction. We never saw the group again and now, knowing they were from Dachau, I doubt they survived the winter.

When I was captured in late November of 1944, I weighed about 155 pounds. It would have been interesting to know my weight at the time of our release in late April of 1945 but I would estimate my weight was about 100 pounds.

In early February of 1945 the Germans moved large numbers of POWs from other locations in Germany to other camps, one of which was Stalag VIIA in Moosburg. A large number of these POWs were from Luft III, a camp near Sagan, Poland. They had endured a long journey by foot and boxcars in extreme cold and with little food or water for such an ordeal. Among those who made the journey from another camp to Moosburg was a friend David Workman, of Stanton, with whom I became acquainted after I married my wife, who had been raised in Stanton. David Workman was a bombardier, flying in a B-17s from Italy when he was shot down over Germany.

April 29, 1945, will always be a date to remember, not only by myself, but all of the POWs interned in Stalag VIIA. I wish I could have kept a diary of all of the events I was involved with during WWII, but it would have been foolhardy to record daily life prior to my capture. We were cautioned, in no uncertain terms, not to have any papers with us after we went on line in France for in the event of capture by the enemy, we would not offer information that might be valuable. After I was captured I did not have, nor could obtain, writing materials.

At the time I was captured in late November of 1944, the Germans took all of the small amount of money from my wallet, leaving me a receipt for what appeared to be in the amount of fifty cents. I was able to retain my wallet with all else intact. I did have a small address book, which measured about two by three inches, in which I recorded the following in pencil, smudged and difficult to decipher after fifty some years:

> **March 25, 1945**: Heard that the final
> big push had started—that Stuttgart
> had fallen—heard yesterday that

> airborne had landed there—Allies supposed to be near Nurnberg. Heard that (?) had made a speech..war over in two weeks. Open the door and give me a shovel!

We were asked one day in late March of 1945, to volunteer to unload a freight car filled with Red Cross parcels. I was happy to have the chance to have something different to do and was one of the volunteers. There must have been twenty or twenty-five of us unloading the parcels when, either by accident or by design, one of our men dropped a parcel causing it break open, spilling the contents. Most of us, including myself, looked upon this as a windfall and hurriedly filled our pockets with the loose foodstuff. The guards yelled like crazy and demanded we return the items, separating those suspected of picking up the items from those who did not. I was in the group of those who were not noticed. I decided keeping the items was not the right thing to do and gave up my meager horde of sugar cubes I had secreted in my clothes. The guards then placed me in the group who were guilty of picking up the items. Hence, I was put in the sonder barracks, confined to the building, prohibited from having Red Cross items and fed only bread and water. This was lucky for me in the respect that I had contacted mumps and now was able to stay off my feet. The notes from the small address book continue....

March 31, 1945: Second day of what I believe will be 14 in Sonder Barracks.

Apr 1, 1945: It's not so bad. What the heck.. I could be back with the fellows—sure hope I don't get my stuff stolen. Nothing to do but eat and sleep...what little I get— 1/2 loaf of bread. Wish I had a diary or something. I haven't thought so much of home since I was at Ludwigsburg.

Apr 3, 1945: This morning the Jerry cap. called us out & sentenced us to 30 days. Told us we would get court martialled after the war.

Apr 9, 1945: Thursday 5, we were all cleared out of the Sonder Barracks to make room for more new coming into the camp. We learned that all pvts. and NCOs were to be moved—where beats me. I was up to see the British Cap. Fri—told me I have the mumps—just a light case—doesn't bother me at all. Everyone is very optimistic about the war. General opinion is that an attack is headed in this direction.

We were all moved to what was known as the "north larger" from the isolierbracken where we were able to join some British soldiers. I found the British army privates more likable than the British noncoms who were housed in Barracks #53 as they were congenial and down to earth. Some of these British soldiers were Ivan Freestone, Fred Hutson, Fred Sharpe and J.W. Pickin. Also, we were able to trade across the single layer fence with some POWs from India. The Indian soldiers were allowed almost unlimited freedom in the area and were wonderful to obtain some items in exchange for cigarettes. I found the Indian soldiers to be very honest as you could trust them with cigarettes and they always came back to our location with either bread or would return the cigarettes.

During the long days of inactivity in the North Larger, I met and conversed at length with an Indian soldier named Armin Ghafur. Before we parted company he wrote me a "letter" on a piece of paper which he probably would have preferred to use as toilet paper. Actually, I do not believe the people of India used toilet paper, although I did not discuss this practice with Ghafur.

Ghafur's letter...

Armin Ghafur. V. Hamid. P.O (Drer)
HAZPO, Dist. Campbell Pore, Punjab, India

1. The only thing which I will miss when I am away from here will be the "Sweet American"

2. When I reach my on home I will tell the Old Girl (my Mother) that the American tank brought the "Happiest"
day of my life April the twenty-ninth, 45.
Freedom! Freedom! Freedom after hard long starving nights of the miserable "Gefengened life."
Good on you America.

3. The Gerry is kaput now.

30/4/45 A Ghafur
Moosburg, Germany

...my notes continue...

Apr 11, 1945: Bombers been flying over for about 15 minutes—saw a few fighters too—looks very good. Moved again yesterday—over in the North Larger now with a group of non-workers.

Apr 18, 1945: Heard yesterday that patrols had reached Nurenburg—been hearing rumbling bombs over Augsburg. Opinion seems to be equally divided also on question of whether we'll be moved or not when they get close. Heard a couple of days ago (12th?) that Roosevelt had died—seems to be true.

Apr 24, 1945: They're supposed to be at Reinsburg now (*I cannot read the name of the town correctly..it only looks like Reinsburg*). Planning a new drive on Munich. We are in their path. Sooner the better. A guy can't tell what's liable to happen. Heard that Augsburg fell early this morning. Moosburg supposed to be declared open city.

Apr 26, 1945: For the last three days have been hearing rumors that the Jerry guard is going to take off on us, leaving only a few American officers to take over management. They're getting closer all the time. I heard rumors that they're shelling Landshut.

May 1, 1945: I am now a free man—in many ways I am more of a prisoner. Morning of 29 Apr, about 6:30, we heard a burst of machine gun fire to the NW of North Larger—didn't think too much about it although it did sound like an American gun and we knew that they were fairly close. About

9:00 we heard a fire fight to the west of Moosburg. Lookout on guard tower next reported that he saw a couple of tanks and trucks. Fire fight moved further west into Moosburg. Soon all was quiet. Jerry guard came down just after lookout reported 4 jeeps came into main larger and called all Jerry guards into main larger *(camp)*. The whole compound packed gate waiting to see a jeep and G.I.s American flag was raised at 12:50 PM at main gate. A great cheer arose from the throng. Shortly after arriving G.I.s walked into a gate about 100 yards up toward the main gate and waved to us and we cheered a few minutes. Later spoke to a Lieutenant for a few minutes. At 4 on

Apr. 30, I saw my first American girl in about 9 months—cute! Nearly a riot!

••

In recent years I have read more than one report or story concerning the actual liberation of Stalag VIIA by Patton's 14th Armored Division. In a book written by Kenneth Simmons, supposedly General George Patton sent a staff car under a white flag to Moosburg to negotiate the surrender of the camp. According to his story, a meeting was held but the German commandant turned down Patton's request to surrender at the insistence of a colonel in the S.S. who was present with the German delegation. An American general, Major General Smith, a member of Patton's staff, then informed the German delegation they would attack at 8:00 AM the next morning. The ensuing fight for the camp and Moosburg included fighter planes strafing the guard towers.

Another report obtained from the interrogations of former POWs, told a slightly different story of the same event. In this story, the contact between the commandant of the German forces and Patton's Division was initiated by the Germans, sending a vehicle occupied by two Swiss representatives, the German commandant, an officer from the S.S. and a British representative from the POWs to the American lines. After a meeting with a general from Patton's Division, the plan was rejected by the American general. Immediately after the vehicle returned to Moosburg and the prison camp, the battle started. This report of the battle of short duration does not mention the use of fighter planes, but does mention the death of one POW which happened, according to the story, when a shell hit a barracks.

My recollection agrees with the notes which I made on the day after the liberation in my little address booklet. I was in the North larger at the time, which was next to a large cultivated field containing potatoes. That morning I saw a German soldier running across the field, heading away from the advancing American forces, carrying what looked like an ammunition box, but no rifle. I remember hearing the small arms fire, which included the sounds of burp guns firing and the slower BARs of the Americans, but do not remember hearing the sound of cannon fire. I certainly would have remembered fighter planes strafing the guard towers. However, earlier there was smaller plane, such as a Piper Cub spotter, flying over the camp.

At any rate, we were free and we were very happy!

<u>WESTERN UNION TELEGRAM</u>

DL5 23 GOVT=WUX WASHINGTON DC JUNE 3 521P

MRS. ESTHER I LINDSEY

1103 SOUTH CHINA ST BRADY TEX=

THE SECRETARY OF WAR DESIRES ME TO INFORM YOU THAT YOUR SON PVT LINDSEY ADRIAN L RETURNED TO MILITARY CONTROL 29 APR 45=

J A UL10 THE ADJUTANT GENERAL

CHAPTER SEVEN

FREEDOM
&
THE TRIP HOME

V-Mail letter, dated may 14, 1945, France. The return address is: Pvt. A.L. Lindsey 38559376, RAMP, 1103 S. China, Brady, Texas. (*This was written from Le Havre, France, Camp Lucky Strike, while waiting for ship back to the States)*

Dearest Mater,

No doubt you may congratulate your one year departed son upon being very lucky. He is well and walking about of own free motive power once again after being cooped up--grand feeling! And that isn't all--rumor's are that he's gonna get a furlough of sixty days to spend at his leisure--home and your cooking. You may tell the bakery to expect a sudden run on doughnuts--better stock up yourself on ingredients for hotcakes and angel food cakes that you can throw together so lovely. 'Gonna make up for that birthday cake that I never received. When?--don't know exactly yet--middle of June if lucky

Love ya, Bud

WESTERN UNION TELEGRAM

DH 14 42 GOVT=WASHINGTON DC JUNE 19 1120P

MRS ESTHER I LINDSEY=

1103 SOUTH CHINA ST BRADY TEX=

THE CHIEF OF STAFF OF THE ARMY DIRECTS ME TO INFORM YOU THAT YOUR SON PVT LINDSEY ADRIAN L IS BEING RETURNED TO THE UNITED STATES WITHIN THE NEAR FUTURE AND WILL BE GIVEN AN OPPORTUNITY TO COMMUNICATE WITH YOU UPON ARRIVAL=

J A ULIO THE ADJUTANT GENERAL

I don't know if the young American girl, who showed up at Stalag VIIA only two days after we were overrun by the American forces, was in uniform or not. She may have been some type of correspondent or with the Red Cross. Needless to say, there was quite a throng of smelly, dirty and otherwise uncouth POWs crowded around.

There is a name in my little address book, Mary Small, ARC, from Boston, Massachusetts. This could have been the young lady and she must have been from the American Red Cross, thus the acronym "ARC" in my book after her name.

I was told, or perhaps read in an account of the events of April 29, 1945, that the Red Cross showed up with doughnuts and American coffee. If this is true, I missed the whole thing. Certainly I would have remembered being offered a doughnut.

The action of the American tank which ran through the main gate at Stalag VIIA that morning on April 29, 1945, was only symbolic as the camp guards had all but ceased their duties as guards of POWs. For the last few days the guards in the North Larger had been letting groups of POWs out into a potato field which bordered the camp to dig potatoes. They would count off a group, let them through the fence, then count them back in.

General Patton visited Stalag VIIA soon after the American forces overran the camp. He was sporting his famous pearl-handled six-shooters and speaking, so I heard, in rather graphic language when referring to the Germans, stating he was going to whip certain parts of their blankety-blank anatomies all the way to Berlin. I did not see the General during his visit.

After the excitement of our release ebbed somewhat many of the former POWs took a tour of the small town of Moosburg, one of which was myself. A few of the newly freed men evidently found something to drink stronger than the local water, commandeered the local fire truck and drove around town yelling and taking on. What I really wanted more than anything else was a slice or two of white bread, but none was available. The arriving American forces were not equipped to feed or otherwise take care of the problems involved with such a great number of men, though the individual soldiers handed out what supplies they had with them.

My trip to town ended with my taking (some called it "liberating") some picture post cards from a two-story house. I am not proud of my actions and have tried to locate the owner of these keepsakes to no avail. I wrote a letter to the "burger master" of Moosburg many years ago, enclosing some Xerox copies of the pictures, explaining I wished to locate the owner as they might be family keepsakes. I received no reply nor was my letter returned. Perhaps my addressing the letter to "the burger master" caused it to be delivered to the nearest MacDonalds outlet.

After the introduction of the internet, I found Moosburg had a web site partly devoted to the Stalag VIIA facility. The Germans in charge of the web site responded to my request and wished to help in my quest for the owner of these items. I supplied the name, Sebastian Trini, which appeared on one of the postcards to the Germans who operate the web site. They e-mailed four possible addresses in Germany to which I wrote, sending copies of some of the pictures from the Moosburg residence. So far I have not received an answer to my inquiries. The search continues.

This web site was also helpful in trying to locate the young lad who found three toothbrushes in Munich but missed our work group. I did receive a letter from a man with the name of Herman B. Reischbock, who now lives in Munich, and though the ages agreed, he was living in another town in 1945 and was not the young man with the toothbrushes in 1945.

••••••••••••••••••••••••••

A short time after we were released and after our trip to the town of Moosburg, I went over to a building which was located across the road and near Stalag VIIA. It contained some type of machine shop equipment but I have no idea of its use. I stood on a little bridge over a small stream and just watched the water. Shortly a Russian recently released POW joined me, watching the water move under the bridge. We did not converse as neither of us knew the other's language, but nodded and smiled to each other, I think understanding each other without words.

The Russian prisoners had a rough time as POWs compared to those from countries who were members of the Geneva Accord prior to WWII. As they did not receive the Red Cross parcels supposedly they received double the normal rations which the American and British POWs received; i.e., instead of five men sharing a loaf of the German bread there would be only two or three. Instead of receiving a eight ounce cup of soup, they should have received fifteen or sixteen ounces of soup, hardly a fair trade for the nutritious Red Cross parcels.

The following is a letter from Doyle Borchers, Box 294, Clifton, Texas, addressed to 1103 South China, Brady. He was a fellow prisoner. Several of us moved from the camp across the road and found a room in a building that had straw for a floor in a small room. I was sick, running fever and Doyle Borchus brought me water and found some food. My sickness was not the remnants of the mumps, but probably was some type of virus which did not last but a couple of days. Although the American forces did have medical care for the seriously ill, they were hard pressed for a short period of time being able to take care of the great number of prisoners.

Doyle Borchers wanted me to hitchhike across Germany and France to La Havre, but I declined. I waited for transportation provided by the Army later. This letter clears up some questions in my mind.

Postmark Clifton, Texas, July 5, 1945, 4PM.

Well Lindsey,

It has taken quite a while for me to get around to this but? Well at any rate the important thing is that I have.

Boy oh! boy I was really puzzled when I got that box with that most valuable shaving brush.

As you know I called your mother shortly after I came home (collect of course)

You are probably wondering about what happened to me after I left. Well the evac hosp. they took me to right after I left was right outside of Moosburg & I stayed there for several days and then V.E. day we were taken to Landhsut in ambulances to the air strip & we flew to Swendel, England about

60 miles from London then after three or four more hospitals we were flown to northern Scotland & we flew to Iceland, New Foundland then landing in New York. Guess you know how that felt. We were at the Santanil Gen. Hosp. two days and then they flew me to Waco & out to McCloskey Gen. Hosp. where I am stationed as a patient. They have fixed up a brace for my foot & I am good as new. I am on a 60 day convalescent leave now and my Dr. said if I felt like another 30 days just to let him know. But he also mentioned that I may be able to get a discharge so I think I will go back right after the 60 so I can find out what's what. But you know how it is.

Have really been enjoying everything.

About the picture of your little sister I will send it soon as I can get it fixed up.

I am also writing Raymond K. & will send his picture also.

Be sure & write now & tell me everything that happened since I left & what happened to the colonels

Your Friend, Doc. Tex.

The reference to the picture of my little sister (Mary Ellen) in the letter from Doyle Borchers answers a question that I had. I had no idea how I was able to get the picture painted by the French artist back to the States as we had nothing but the clothes on our backs and no way to carry such a thing as a picture. Evidently I gave the picture to Doyle for him to bring back.

I had the chance to visit Doyle Borchers at Lake Whitney, which is located just a short distance from Clifton, some years later. He was involved in local politics and was County Attorney I believe at the time of our visit.

We were moved by army trucks to a landing strip not too far from Moosburg where we boarded C-47s which had been equipped with bucket seats. I do not remember getting on the plane (which bothers me as this was the first time I had flown). I do remember the flight across the mountains in route to an airstrip outside of Paris as being very bumpy and very uncomfortable as I had little padding on my posterior.

We were then trucked to Le Havre, France, to a tent city known as Lucky Strike. By this time the war in Europe was over and it was really nice to have our trucks, which were transporting us to Le Havre, driving with full headlights.

At Le Havre we were issued some clothing and one of those sleeping bags that were shaped like a human's torso. We had a special name for these bags, one that is not usually spoken in polite company. It was awfully cold in Le Havre I suppose because we had such little body fat. I could not eat very much, my eyes being much larger than my stomach. One morning I went to chow for breakfast and it made me sick. We would gradually get back in shape and regain some body weight but it would not happen overnight.

The troops waiting to go back to the States, along with myself, caught a Liberty Ship home and landed at New York. It was a glorious sight to sail past the Statue of Liberty and I feel sure that some of us shed a tear or two. It was wonderful to see the fire boats in the New York harbor all spraying fountains of water to greet this returning ship of POWs.

We had transportation to Fort Sam Houston, San Antonio, Texas, where I found, much to my amazement, the fellow who ran the cafe just down the street from the Cobb's Drug Store in Brady who had never left Fort Sam—there he was cooking at the mess hall, a profession in high demand. He gave me a fist full of gasoline ration coupons to use while on furlough.

Dad, Mom and my sisters drove from Brady to San Antonio, a distance of perhaps 125 miles, to pick me up at Ft. Sam and we had a joyous reunion. I think the war time speed limit of 35 MPH was still in effect so it was a slow trip, but that was OK by me and the other passengers.

I spent all of my 60 days (I believe it was 60 days)

mostly in Brady. At the same time old friends J.B. Wright and Omar Parker were also on leave. I was in Brady when they announced the dropping of the two atomic bombs and the cessation of hostilities with Japan.

It was certainly great to be back in the States and especially back home in Brady. It was a pleasure to drive slowly around Brady in Dad's 1936 Ford (black in color, of course), a change from when, prior to the war, I would take the only vehicle the family owned and see how fast it would go. I found the top speed was 85 MPH, with no head or tail wind and with all windows rolled up. I never confessed to Dad about my speed trials with the Ford.

Sometime during the furlough, I hitchhiked to Alice, Texas, to visit Harold Davis who was also on leave at that time. Harold also ended up in Europe and had been captured by the Germans.

I found that my body was not as strong as my mind advised. There was a mesquite tree stump in the back yard of my family's home in Brady, I decided to dig it out one morning. I found, in spite of my positive mental state, I could not do so.

While in Brady on my 60-day furlough I received a letter from a former teacher, Miss Laurie Barfoot. Miss Barfoot was the subject of many discussions at class reunions as we all remembered her very well as she was what I would call a "no nonsense" teacher. She would not tolerate any frivolous activity in her classroom and demanded we learn her subject — English. Miss Barfoot seemed ageless, being neither old nor young, but she must have been about 35 years of age in 1942. She was not a pretty woman, nor even handsome, being overweight, but not obese. She was not really liked nor was she disliked. But she had all of the student's respect. This is the letter which I had saved for over 50 years:

Envelope: To: Pvt. Adrian L. Lindsey:
Brady, Texas (*no zip or street address. It has a 3¢ stamp)*

The letter:

Box 650
Stephenville, Texas
June 22, 1945
Dearest Adrian, (*Miss Barfoot was one of the few people to call me Adrian, rather than "Bud"*)

There are dishes to wash and weeds to chop at my house, but when I read my Brady paper and saw that you are safe at home, I dropped everything to write you a line or two. To say that I am happy to know that you are at home would be putting my sentiment very mildly. We have all been so worried about you and our other Brady boys that it is certainly a relief to know that at least a few of you are safe at last.

Do you suppose that a two-months furlough will give you enough time to catch up on all your eating, sleeping, and having fun? You will find Hot Springs, Arkansas, a pretty place when you go there. I had a very nice nine-day trip through scenic Arkansas and its Ozarks one summer. My "tour" included a $1.25 bath at one of the government bath houses there. It was fun.

I was sorry to learn that you had to trade off your B.H.S. ring, but weren't you glad that you had something those kraut-eating Nazis would trade for? It certainly makes me feel bad to know that you were that hungry when we were all so well fed over here, but maybe your mother's good cooking will help you to forget those bad months.

I judge that you missed the tornado. Wasn't that an unexpected calamity for Brady?

I was glad to read that you were helped by the Red Cross. That's what we want them to do with our hard-earned dollars.

I was telling my mother about your experience, and she said that she was going to increase her *monthly payments to the Red Cross. Maybe you can tell people enough about the Germans that some of us will be willing to see them punished so severely that they cannot promote another war within a few months.*

My eldest army-brother is on Okinawa. You can imagine how much we'd like to hear some good news from him. My middle brother was injured in the Italian theater and we expect him to receive a disability discharge. The youngest one is taking a special eight-weeks course for officers at Fort Leavenworth.

I'm a very insignificant American citizen, but I'd like to thank you for what you have done and will do in serving our country. Enjoy your furlough.

With love and best wishes,

Laurie Barfoot

I do not know if Miss Barfoot wrote any of the other service men or their families, but I suspect she did. Perhaps she wrote the parents and family of Houston Lee Braly of Brady, one of her students in the class of 1941, one class ahead of me. He and his family were friends of mine. His father ran a small dairy outside of Brady and I purchased milk from him for the soda fountain at Cobb's Drug.

Houston was piloting a fighter in France, following another plane on a strafing run on a German train. The first plane hit the train and caused a massive explosion as the train was evidently filled with munitions. Unfortunately Houston's aircraft flew into the debris and crashed, killing Houston. The French citizens of the village recovered Houston's body and hid it from the Germans who arrived to search the area. They then gave Houston a proper burial.

The train explosion also blew the stained glass windows from the church and a movement was started after the war to raise money to replace the church windows. This project has been finished only recently, with a dedication at the France village which Alice Braly, Houston's sister, attended.

At our 50th year class reunion I found that Miss Barfoot, now in her late 80s, was a resident at a Stephenville, Texas, care center. We obtained a poster board, copied our pictures from one of the annuals, pasted them on the board and all signed and wrote messages to Miss Barfoot. One of our classmates lived in Stephenville and volunteered to deliver the completed poster board.

Not long after the class reunion I made it a point to

stop by the care center to visit with Miss Barfoot, expecting to surprise her. I found directions to her room and spotted her in a wheel chair with the poster board prominently displayed on her room's wall.

I said to her, "Miss Barfoot, I am Adrian Lindsey, one of your students from 1942." She asked for me to repeat, which I did.

"I don't remember you," she said.

"Surely you remember me. I was one of your best students and the best looking," I jokingly told her.

"I'm sorry. I don't remember you."

I was disappointed, but I understood I should have visited her earlier and told her I appreciated her urging me in high school and not accepting slip-shod work from me as a student.

School teachers are generally underpaid and put up with a lot of paper work, criticism from the parents and apathy from the students. They have a terrible job trying to sell, bribe and threaten their students into learning something they wish not to do, for use in their distant future to which they cannot relate. Perhaps the greatest reward a teacher can receive is having one of her students return to thank her or him for their teaching efforts after they have experienced years of living in the real world, an action which I procrastinated and failed to do .

I had a few dreams, not so much about being a POW but being with the company on line. One recurring dream was about myself and others confronting a German road block where an eighty-eight was pointed directly at me. I struggled, in each dream, to reach the safety of the ditch alongside of the road. I never knew if I made the ditch or not as the dream ended. The number of times I had had the dream I do not know, but luckily there were not many and they soon disappeared. I do not know why I would dream such a dream as such a circumstance never happened —— a dream which was fabricated in my mind in a dream as might have happened, but didn't.

I reported back to duty to Hot Springs, Arkansas for a short period of R & R.

Postmark Hot Springs National Park, Ark., Aug 21, 1945, 5:30 PM. *The letter was written on stationery purloined from the large hotel, The Arlington Hotel and Baths, but my address was at the Majestic Hotel, Room 676, A.G. & S.F. R. Station.*

Dear Pater,

I went down to finance & got paid yesterday afternoon so here's the 25 I owe--thanks a lot. I was really broke, but that's really nothing unusual--got scads now.

I had not received any pay since before I left the States to go overseas in September of '44. It is now August of '45. Of course, I didn't need any money during that period as there wasn't anything to buy with money. The letter continues...

I took a physical exam this morning. I had my sinuses X-rayed to see if I had sinus trouble--I seem to be in good shape--don't know what kind of a job I'll get. It'll be I.R.T.C. cadre duty. I'd rather do something else, but outdoor work is what I'd like--probably what I'll get too.

Gonna take a typing test this afternoon--right now I'm gonna go eat.

Write, Bud

I guess I felt rather "well to do" after I received all of my back pay as I had not received any pay since we left New York except for some "script" money for use after we landed in France. This would mean I received about nine months of pay, most of it being combat pay.

Postmark Hot Springs National Park, Ark., Aug 25, 1945, 5:30 PM. Return address AG. & S.F. R. Station, majestic Hotel, Room 676, Hot Springs, Ark. Letter dated Aug 25-45, Sat. Morning

Dearest Mom,

In this special instance it was O.K. to read my love (?) letters--Carolyn. It is a funny case. I'll write to Adrian one of the days to see if he is a relative. *(I do not remember what this was about, but perhaps some mail was delivered to an "Adrian" at Brady)*

Well I'm all through with everything--classes, physical, etc. I'll lay around until about Monday then go to Camp Crowder, Missouri, near Joplin in the southwest corner near the Okla. line. I talked my way into radio training & if I keep talking when I get there I'll get it. They offered me a job pounding a typewriter (I didn't even ask them where---I'd go crazy doing that). I have sinus trouble the x-rays show so no more infantry line work nor overseas duty.

There's hardly a chance of getting out unless they lower the points. I did find out that I have another battle star---5 points.

I stopped by & saw Jo & Alice a little bit--Ken should be home within a few days. I phoned the Walker's but no one was home so I let it go.

And I thought I could sew--I went down to the USO the other night -- I took a bunch of pants up but when I tried to alter a shirt--wow! I got one side of one fixed then quit--next time I'm home I want you to teach me something.

gotta go eat, Love, Bud

The brief stay in Hot Springs was pleasant. The Army had arranged for horseback rides, dances and other types of entertainment. We did not have any regular Army duties during this time, only to take tests and physicals. I was gaining my weight back and, aside from the fact I was not very strong, generally felt very good.

Postmark Camp Crowder, MO, Aug 29, 1945, 11:30 AM. Letter dated Aug 28-45, Tues. night. Return address: P.F.C. A. Lindsey, 38559376, Co. D, 35 Sig. Bn., Camp Crowder, Mo. Via Air Mail (eight cent stamp)

Dearest Mom,

This is far from being a love letter--I feel sorta bitter today for lots of reasons. This is really some place (sarcasm)--the camp (buildings, etc.) is typically nice enough but the system is awful. I guess I haven't been back to the grind in so long that it's kinda a shock. They talk a lot about a G.I. being trouble converting into a civilian--'twon't be anything like coming off of a 60 day furlough & going back to the old grind.

We got in at 5 this morning & were awakened at 6--we had hoped to get some sleep but no such luck. I won't be here permanently--only about three weeks more or less. I've about decided to heck with radio & get a job pounding a typewriter. I can't get exactly what I want in radio I don't think. I'll just have to wait & see. I don't want to be a radio operator and I think that's all I can get in this man's army.

I checked my baggage & didn't even have a toothbrush until this afternoon when I went over to the PX. I can't find a towel in camp so I will shake myself like a dog & apply the laws of evaporation until I get my baggage. I can't get it out of supply until I'm up for a clothing check which may be several days. Some place..

Mom, sometimes I wonder if I'll ever amount to anything or not. I won't have much to go on after I get out--most of all be able to do anything specialized. Right now I'd like more than anything to marry Dot, but I know that's no good. You'd live in a single room--get off at five in the afternoon until about five the next morning--it's no good--even if she was out of school. Maybe someday if she doesn't forget all about me.

It makes me mad. Two guys brought their wives with them--they had to leave them in the camp bus station until they could check in--they made arrangements for a pass to go to town between 5 & 7 this morning & were lucky enough to find a room. They can't get out tonight because they had to have an application for a pass in before 1 PM for tonight. When I get to be president I'm gonna bust a lot of generals...poor girls.

Bitter me, Bud

Postmark Camp Crowder, Mo, Sept 1, 1945, 11:30 AM. Letter dated Aug 31-45

Dearest mater,

Things don't look so bad now--maybe I'm getting used to it all. Anyway I'm pretty sure I'll be moved out of the camp--that's good. I kinda think I'll (be) a little closer to home anyway.

And I finally got some mail at noon today--Jack, you, & three from Dot today. What's this about Howard getting out--tell me more! He a lucky guy. I'd like to be out & get something good to do. Jackson's all eager to get out--he really doesn't say much. I'll bet he moves on to Japan. He's very happy that the war's over.

Yes, save that Red Cross box--I'll eat next time I'm home. They tell us at Hot Springs that we would get a furlough but won't here. I'll get one Xmas if I have to create one myself. I can have noon Sat. (tomorrow) until Tues. 6 AM off but I won't try to go down. I'd just be there a few hours--all my clothes are dirty--have to do our own laundry. I don't know what I'll do--just hang around this dump I guess--may go into Joplin & go swimming 'or something'

Love, Bud

I do not know about the Red Cross box. Obviously it was in existence, but I do not know how I ended up with it.

Postmark Camp Crowder, Mo, Sept 13, 1945, 1 PM. Letter dated Sept. 12-45, 9:15 PM

Dearest Mater,

O.K. lady so I've be neglecting you. I'll try to improve a little. I'm sorta temperamental when it comes to writing. My mood varies with the weather and occupation. It's the weather tonight that makes me write. It's been raining all day and it's very cool tonight. Bob and I went over to the show--wore our Mackinaw (short overcoat).

So far nothing's happened--my chances of getting out of this Army are rather impossible right now. I have 39 points now (maybe 40)--the only way I could get out would be to go crazy--get run over by a truck--maybe I could get out on the former. There should be some orders on me sometime this week--next week for sure. I'll be moved into the 8th service command in all probability. This covers Texas,

Louisiana and part of Okla. (I think).

Be nice to be at Camp Bowie--Barkley--Hood--or Ft. Sam. Be nice to be at Ft. Hays, Ohio, too.

Yes, everything seems to be under control in Ohio--if I can just keep it that way till I can go up. I guess you know I'm going up first time I get a chance.

I'm very glad to hear about cuz Chandler--hope he gets out quick. The way things are moving a guy can become a 30 year man just waiting around at a separation center for a discharge.

Adrian doesn't have much to say--or didn't you know. I can just see those two sisters of mine steaming the flaps open on all my mail.

I'm glad to hear that Pater is doing so well--he worries too much I think.

I may not phone but I'll let you know as soon as anything happens.

Love, Bud

Postmark New Orleans, La, Sep 20, 1945, 1:30 PM. Letter dated Sept 19-45, Wednesday. Return address, PFC Adrian L. Lindsey, 38559376, Co B, 22 Bn, 5th Regt. Camp Plauche, Louisiana.

Dearest Mom,

Worst has come to worse all right--never thought I'd be in Louisiana--but! I'm about eight miles from New Orleans, that's something.

And it looks like I'll be here a little while anyway--probably as long as I'm in the Army--which will be a long time, no doubt. First I have to go through the inevitable three day processing then move somewhere else on the post--there's always a chance to be moved off the post but good things never happen to me.

I got this writing kit the day I left--thanks for sending it. I sent that roll of film off before I left so it'll probably be there in ten days or two weeks.

We got some very old fashioned and dirty coaches to come down on (two nights) so I'm just getting all the coal dust off of me. I'm sorta tired--I'll be in a better mood in the morning. All I can say is I don't like it--but I knew that before I got here. The weather is damp & hot--the mosquitoes numerous & big.

Love, Bud

Postmark New Orleans, La., Sep 27, 1945, 7 PM. Letter dated Sept 27, Thursday AM. Return address: Co B, 1st Bn., 1 Regt, Bks 29-5, Camp Plauche, New Orleans, La.

Dearest Mom,

I'm getting lazier all the time--I went up to personnel last night to start this assignment rolling. I still don't know what I'm going to do. Wanted to give me a typing job but I told them "nix"--may have to take it anyway--next time you see me I'll be raving mad, I guess.

I got a letter from Jackson yesterday--he'll probably be in the occupation for awhile--China maybe he says. I hate that--I'd give anything if he and I could get out at the same time.

It looks like I may be able to get out in Jan-Feb or March. Of course, you can't tell.

I'll be getting a furlough before Xmas. I may not get one Xmas but by taking one early the next one will be sooner if I'm still in. Anyway I want you to pack that Eisenhower blouse (O.D. blouse) that's in the closet. It doesn't need cleaning or anything.

Pack it so it won't get wrinkled--wait till I send you my new address and then mail it immediately. Thanks.

What are Howard & Jean doing these days--I'll bet they're happy about the whole thing.

More later--nothing ever happens--I haven't been into town yet. I've been trying to save money. Will get paid in a few days--that's good. I'll probably have to cash a war bond or three or four if I get that furlough. I've got a lot of trading. I'll try to ride a C-47. I'll come back by home. I can't stay but just a couple or three days--be glad when I get home for good. My future seems sorta settled for 4 or 5 months. After that I don't know. I'd like to go down to Andy's ranch & work for a month next summer. I really would. I'd like to do a lot of things but they all conflict with each other.

Love, Bud

Postmark New Orleans, La, Oct 11, 1945, 1:30 PM. Return address: Co B, 4th Bn., 1st regt. Letter dated Oct 11-45, Thurs.

Dearest Pater,

Gee, it's rush-rush-rush now. I'm so used to rarely getting up in the morning to eat chow then going back to sleep that I seem never to have enough time--so darn many things to do after retreat, too.

This training does seem sorta superfluous now that the war is over. Still the fellows will get the same training as before. It's a lot easier than when I came in--little things, you know. My job is assist. platoon sgt. I'm wearing corporal strips but not getting paid for it--getting a rating around here is like asking for the CO's right arm it seems. I may get the pay later.

If not I'll stop doing a good (?) job and be a general sad sack.

Right now I'm going to N.C.'s school--doesn't seem to be what I'd expect of such a school. Never do anything. We've been studying the psychology of teaching. Nutz!

I got the blouse that Mater sent and the iron cord--really needed an iron but the guy across the hall has one that I use & save money that way. I got the money order yesterday and went into town last night to cash it and get some travelers checks. P.S. had a fairly good time, too. My furlough will be in December--the way it is I probably won't have time to go deer hunting--how I'd like too. Maybe we can get us a jeep and good camping equipment and go next winter. I think that's a good idea about the scope--I'd like to get my hands on it. We train with '03s--never had one in my hands. I don't think I'll have a carbine.

About that radio--I didn't really need it. I have a room all by myself, If you'd send me that other one I could bring it back when I get out (next Jan-Feb-Mar-I hope!) by parcel post if possible and you decide to send it. I'd like to have that scarf, too. Oh, I ask for so many things I really don't need them--like to have that scarf though. It's beginning to get cold finally here--had the heat on for the first time last night.

Another thing if it's not too late when you get this--why don't you get Mother to send Jack that parcel that I got back from prison camp--if the contents are appropriate:

P/F. C. J. Kline 974968 USMCR
"L" Co, 3rd Bn, 22nd Mar.
6th Mar Div.

c/o Fleet P.O.
San Francisco, Calif.

I'll bet a dollar that the poor guy is in China now.

Must close & go to school--Cpl. Green across the hall promised to let me carry his books for him...goody, goody, gumdrop.

Your off spring, Bud

Will you check my war bonds and tell me exactly how much cash value they have right now? Thanks,--should be about $1100.00

Postmark: New Orleans, LA, Oct 27, 1945, 1:30 PM. Letter dated Friday noon

Dearest Mom, The pictures were pretty good. Thanks for sending them on. We took more than that--some didn't turn out, others were on the other roll of "Pinkys".

Gee, I don't know, Mom, I'm getting thoroughly disgusted. You yell all day and it doesn't seem to do a heck of a lot of good. I feel just like standing back and laughing at the whole thing.

What I need is a furlough--good and long. It will come up on November rather than December now. Some of the guys are getting discharged that were ahead of me. I wish I had a car.

Yesterday was really a miserable day--cloudy, misting, and windy. Cold too for a change. It gets cold here at night but usually it's nice and clear during the day. I saw a small bunch of geese go over as the company moved out yesterday morning--wish I could get lined up and go goose hunting. Tell Pater I have a Mackinaw (short overcoat) that's going to make a nice hunting coat. I'll keep it one way or another--maybe we <u>can</u> go deer hunting. I'll probably be on furlough about Thanksgiving. I won't have too much time--if I had a car I could do so much better. The way I feel now I would take some extra time.

I haven't heard from Harold--probably won't ever and I don't care..tell you all about it sometime.

gotta fall out in 10 min   Love, Bud

I do not remember why I made this statement about Harold Davis. We were good friends. I just don't remember. Harold and I were in junior high together in Alice, Texas. We both had inquiring minds and were the perpetrators of various projects, one of which was to build our own wheels as borrowing our family cars was very infrequent. We walked to the area metal scrap place to find an axle and wheels of some sort. We then looked carefully at an outboard motor, which belonged to Harold's dad, to be used to propel our vehicle. We knew nothing about what we were doing and did not complete this engineering project which is probably what saved the outboard motor from destruction.

For income, Harold and I delivered the Thursday afternoon grocery circulars for the H.E. Butt grocery store in Alice. We each received 67 1/2¢ for our afternoon's efforts. We were acquainted with every biting dog in that part of town.

The tone of some of the letters from Camp Plauche was negative, however, as far as being in the Army it was OK. We were giving basic training to new inductees who were not too happy about being drafted as many had been in the Merchant Marines. One of the cadre had a Willis four-door sedan and we had many chances to go into New Orleans and see the sights, one of which was Bourbon Street.

I also went on a boat trip up the Mississippi one evening. I believe this paddle-wheeler was called the Delta Queen or something like that and is still in service as a tourist attraction.

Camp Plauche camp was located very close to the Huey Long Bridge and I could walk over, climb the levee and watch the Mississippi roll by, a much larger stream than Brady Creek or the San Saba River in Texas.

Postmark New Orleans, La, Nov 5, 1945, 6:30 PM. Letter dated Nov 4, Sunday, 4:00 PM

Dearest Mom.

Lady, I've sorta lost all track of time it seems--busy all of the time for nothing, too. No pay for the stripes and I probably won't ever get them. I went up to see about getting my combat pay--won't even be able to get that for awhile--nothing has come in on it yet.

I got the radio O.K.. It's great--surely does add a nice touch to this drab barracks. I usually go to sleep every night with it on. Thanks a lot.

I went into town last night--I bought Dot a quilted

white house coat that I can take up to her when I go. I think she needs one--not sure. I'd get her some mules to match when I can find out her shoe size.

What's this about that bronze star--there must be some mistake. Lady, the 20th of Nov but may wait until December for a furlough. If I take it in Nov I'd have to come back about the 15 of December. I might get a chance to get three four or five days off at Xmas anyway. I don't know yet--I'll let you know. Depends on Dot and whether I get a car or not.

Pater, I'd hate to miss a deer hunt. I went out on a 50ft .22 range the other day--I'm not quite as nervous as I thought I was. We used .22s just like we have with a Weaver peep rear sights--"Matchmasters" aren't they?

I couldn't get my eye down to the peep on the standing position so I sorta shot them from the hip--I'm from Texas you know.

Write.. Love, Bud

(Enclosed with this letter were cut-outs from four targets showing the results of the shooting range.)

Postmark New Orleans, La, Nov 19, 1945, 2 PM. Letter dated Nov 18-45, Sunday afternoon. This letter was typewritten.

Dear Pater,

Being in a fairly good and congenial mood this afternoon, I'll try to let you in on everything that's been happening to your favorite son.

Up to now all that's happened about discharges is what had been in the paper. The notice has to come down officially. As it is this Camp Plauche seems to be a forgotten place as far as the war dept. is concerned. We'll probably be the the last to get out. When all this will come about it's hard to say. We've been expecting something any day now--maybe this coming week. When we do get the word we may put in our request for discharge and in a few days after they're okayed (they will be) we'll go to the separation center here in camp. I will be out by Xmas I'm certain. I wish that I could have made it by Thanksgiving but that's a little premature.

In view of everything it would be silly for me to take a furlough now. When I do get out I think I'll go up to Ohio with one of the fellows here--see Dot. As for buying a car I don't know whether I will or not. Anyway after a few days in Ohio I'll be ready to go on that deer hunt so try to line up some rifles.

I've been out on the range this last week. Lots of work, and rush-rush all the time. The place is close to the gulf--saw lots of ducks out there...this would be a wonderful place to go duck hunting. I got a chance to fire the '03 for the first time. Also the bazooka. We had fun just playing around. No one was killed---'twas a miracle the way some of these guys handle their rifles.

The craziest things can happen to me. Lt. Whitehead (Platoon leader of my platoon) and I decided that we would fire the '03 transition course--at silhouettes (sp?). About the time we were ready to start a staff car rolled up. As luck would have it a whole stack of brass stepped out and came up to our firing point. He had to get up and report to them and show them what was happening. I couldn't get out of it so I went ahead and fired. I had a rifle that I'd never fired before and wasn't zeroed--I couldn't hit a thing. Lt. Whitehead spun them a line about me being nervous and a long sob story about me being a P.F.C. pulling a sgt.'s job, etc. 'Twas all very funny. I'm known as bolo Lindsey now.

Mom said that you needed a few shorts. In a few minutes I'll go over to the P.X. and see if I can find some that you can wear. Yes, we still have men in the army that wear 38's. *(At the time I wrote this letter I probably had a 28 inch waist line..perhaps smaller)* Also I'm sending some extra clothes and stuff....take care of it all for me--hope to see you soon, Bud

Postmark New Orleans, Nov 23, 1945, 1:30 PM. Letter dated Nov 21-45, Wed afternoon.

Dearest Mom,

Nothing's happened--something soon on discharges I hope. The notice did come down on the daily bulletin, but it has to be better than that. We have our names in--it'll only be a matter of weeks.

Tomorrow is Thanksgiving--I wish I was there to get some of that pumpkin pie, etc. that you will no doubt have.

Mom, I'll be there Xmas even if I have to wait till after to see Dot. I have my whole life ahead.

I looked for those shorts but the largest was 34. I'll try a couple of more PXs over Thanksgiving and send the box on no matter whether I get them or not. I'll also be shipping the radio back in a week or so.

About the "bronze star medal'--it's all a mistake I know without even checking on it. I won't bother. If I did get it I would know about it. For one thing you have to do something for it. Then it's presented in a ceremony. It doesn't matter--I don't need the points.

The document wasn't even signed--they send them all out to members of ye olde 100th who were on the approach to the Rhine or in Central Germany.

Darn! It rained real hard while I was at chow--I came back and there was a big puddle in the middle of the bed--all over the room for that matter. I had just brought in some dry clothes off the line--back they went. Never seem to get ahead in man's army!

More later. Love ya, Bud

••••••••••••••••••••

That was the end of letters home. My discharge came through.

CHAPTER EIGHT

OUT OF THE ARMY

...ONCE AGAIN A CIVILIAN

As the discharged veteran could choose a destination, transportation paid, to a point of his choice, I chose Columbus, Ohio to visit Dot. Now a world traveler, having gone to Europe and having been yelled and shot at by both sides, I felt I could risk riding the train from New Orleans to Columbus, Ohio, routing through Chicago. I then rode the train returning from Columbus to Ft. Worth without getting lost. As the train was traveling through Illinois, it made a brief stop and a young fellow came down the aisle selling newspapers. He said to the passengers, "Joliet paper! Joliet paper!" I swore he said "toilet paper" and I started to buy some as I had vowed never to run out of that stuff for the rest of my life.

I had met Dot during the 60-day furlough after returning to the States from Europe. She was visiting her brother and sister-in-law in Brady. We were both young, she younger than I, as she was still in high school. After a two day visit in Ohio, I returned to Brady, where not long after I received a "Dear John" letter from Dot. This was OK by me, for after a very short bereavement period, I met a very wonderful young lady in Midland, Texas (she was from nearby Stanton) with whom I intend to spend the rest of my life..

In Brady I received a letter, postmarked August 24, 1945, from the young man in Munich who had tried to obtain three toothbrushes. We had given Ludwig, the young lad, our home addresses. The letter was as follows:

> *Hallo Mr. Lindsey!*
>
> *I want to write you some now. How do you do! I hope, well. I am well too. Are you good come home. I hope so. And now I want remember you at me. I am the boy which has given to you, Mr. Schaefer and Mr. Delano bread for tea. I am sorry, I had get three nice toothbrushes, but you did not more come back that Thursday, I was looking for you all working places. But I am happy now that the war is finest now and you long time at prisoner has a end. I will close now and I hope very much, you write me soon too. Many compliments at your family. Please write soon.*
>
> *Good bye! Your little friend Ludwig.*

I regret I had not tried to contact Ludwig earlier. I did answer his letter, but I did not keep a copy and did not elect to continue the correspondence.

My recent attempts to locate him proved to be futile.

CHAPTER NINE

YEARS LATER

...ABOUT 55 YEARS LATER

Looking back at World War II and my involvement, brief though it was, I think about many things. I worried about such things as leaving the two grenades in the foxhole in the Vosges Mountains. I have often thought of the four Germans in the outpost foxhole who captured me. Certainly the next day or the day after, they would have to confront the advancing troops of the 100th Infantry Division, and would either be captured, killed or perhaps would have a chance to retreat.

I feel badly about misrepresenting the number of cigarettes or the quality of the British tea to the German housewives who were caught up in circumstances over which they had little control.

A member of the armed forces of any country is taught to follow orders without question. This is the very basic foundation of which an army is built and the only chance of its being successful. In spite of this training an individual soldier has some flexibility. The actions of an individual soldier are the result of the way he was brought up and the values he had attained previously. I feel sure the four Germans in the fox hole who captured me in the Vosges Mountains that day were not ordered to shoot rather than capture, but one of the four German soldiers could have easily used me for target practice and nothing would have ever been said of the action.

According to one report made after the war the Germans tried unsuccessfully to separate the Jewish prisoners from the other prisoners. I was not aware of this action and it did not take place in our barracks. Another incident was reported of a Russian prisoner being shot as he tried to escape by climbing the barbed wire fence and was left hanging, wounded. An English prisoner tried to rescue him and was shot, but recovered. The Russian died. I did not witness this event.

One question asked of me many times about being in a German prison camp was if I was mistreated while under the care of the German Army. I have to reply that no, aside from the lack of food, there was no malicious physical abuse. Some reports from other POW camps in Germany indicate some Kriegies were not as fortunate as I. Our morale was generally good, boosted by seeing the progress of the Allied efforts in the sky and hearing the progress on the ground. The prisoners of the Japanese were isolated and were treated harshly. We were not, by reasonable standards of the times.

After arriving home in Brady, I was contacted by an American Army officer, Colonel Robert G. Saxon, who was in charge of a prisoner of war camp for captured German soldiers which was located just outside of Brady. I went out to report to the Colonel Saxon who wished to know how we were treated in Germany. I gave him a factual account and he ordered the rations of the German prisoners to be cut in half. Even with one half rations, the Germans POWs never had it so good. Some of the German prisoners at Brady were from early in the war, probably members of Rommel's African Corps, and were troublesome.

For some time I exchanged Christmas cards with some of the twelve men who made up our "bunk tier" and ration group, but we have gradually lost touch. After discovering the internet I did find the name of Albert Delano, of New Market, Indiana. I picked up the phone, dialed and he answered. Unlike most of the young men of WWII, he still lived in the same town.

Albert Delano had volunteered to become one of a group of volunteers for a work group which operated some miles from Stalag VIIA. This group was housed in a barn, numbering somewhere between fifty and one hundred POWs guarded by fifteen or twenty guards. They had volunteered for the work group in hopes of getting better food. They were put to work repairing a railroad and did complete the repair. Albert told me before any trains could use the newly repaired track, American planes promptly bombed it to make it inoperative.

Delano also told of a German civilian, an older man and a veteran of WWI, who rode a bicycle daily west to check on the progress of the advancing American troops, thus keeping them informed. After Albert was discharged he became postmaster of the post office in his home town of New Market, Indiana.

Stewart Arft was from Pleasant Ridge, Michigan. He and Albert Delano were part of a water-cooled machine gun crew in H Company of the 397th Infantry Regiment which was part of the 100th Infantry Division. They were captured together about the same time I was captured, in late November of 1944. Stewart Arft became a dentist in civilian life and had stayed in touch with Albert Delano.

Ted Doty was from Muncie, Indiana, but went to work for General Electric after the war and lived in Schenectady, New York. He returned to Germany in the early 60s and sent me some pictures of Stalag VIIA at that time.

I worked as a radio broadcast engineer in Midland, Texas, for some years, then went to work for an electronics wholesale firm. In 1969 I started working for the Region 18 Education Service Center in Midland, establishing an audio-visual equipment repair center for the school districts in West Texas. I was also involved, part time, in the filming and processing of 16 mm sports movie film. After I retired, we moved to Stanton in 1991.

Other names I kept in the small address book as being in Stalag VIIA and in our group of the 12-man bunk tier group were; Johnny Dagevais (Detroit, Michigan), Jake Rogers (Saluda, South Carolina), Rudolph Shafer (Beverly Hills, California) and Harold Camp (Dayton, Ohio). We never had a reunion, we POWs, and that is a shame, but it is a time that is past now and cannot be recaptured as many of us are no longer available. There are other names in the book the reason and circumstance of their being carefully written has been long forgotten.

I had saved, along with some other souvenirs, a twenty Reichmark bill which was inscribed with some American names and addresses. I had not looked at these items in about forty years and had no idea of the incident of getting the twenty Reichmark paper money. I certainly did not have the bill in prison camp as the Germans had taken any money I had in my possession, and there would have been no need for such while in Stalag VIIA. The names listed on the paper money were: Dick Cade, Lubbock; Donald C. Stafford, Piedmont, California; John R. Yates, Edwardsville, Illinois; Charles S. Reid, Souderton, Pennsylvania. There was one other name which was not readable.

I had saved the twenty-Reichmark bill for over fifty years. I had no idea who gave me the bill, but it had to be one of the members of the American Army liberating force at the gate of Stalag VIIA, on April 29, 1945. One of the names on the bill was Dick Cade of Lubbock, Texas, whose name appears on the left side of the bottom copy of the front of the bill (above). I had not tried to locate any of the soldiers who signed the bill until December of 2000, when I obtained the phone number of Dick Cade in Slaton, Texas, near Lubbock. Unfortunately, after more than one-half century many things are forgotten and Dick Cade did not remember signing the bill but he certainly remembered the day. So did I.

The internet listed a Dick Cade as living in Slaton, Texas, not far from Lubbock. I had a phone number.

I dialed the number, hoping I had not disturbed someone's Christmas dinner, and his daughter answered. She advised me that it was indeed the residence of Dick, he had served in the army in Europe and he was home. Dick Cade came to the phone and I quickly found he was at Moosburg, Germany at the time. I explained where I had obtained his name and asked if he would be available for a visit and he indicated he would like to visit.

A few days later my wife and I drove to Dick Cades's farm near Slaton, a distance of some ninety miles, and enjoyed a delightful visit with Dick and his wife Catherine.

Dick Cade was in the 99th Infantry Division, 3rd Battalion, Company I, but had been moved to a special guard unit which had been placed around the 99th Division's 395th Regimental Headquarters site. As his division neared the Moosburg area, he, along with others in his guard company, heard of the impending liberation of a prisoner of war camp. They made their way forward and arrived at the camp shortly after the Germans had surrendered. I hoped Dick would remember the twenty Reichmark bill and his signing but he did not, and I was not surprised as it had been about fifty-five years since he signed that note. Dick Cade did tell me he stayed in touch with Donald C. Stafford, one of the other names appearing on the bill.

At Stalag VIIA Dick Cade did find two members of his division who had been taken prisoner earlier, Mathis and Garrison. It was quite a joyous reunion for the group.

Dick Cade's division had entered Europe in northern France after the initial invasion and proceeded to work their way east and south, he surviving The Battle of the Bulge in late 1944. His outfit arrived at Moosburg on April 29, 1945, to assist in the liberation of Stalag VIIA.

I'll never forget that dead German soldier, the first of many I saw, and the futility of his death. It will forever be implanted in my mind the carnage which was experienced by both sides. The bombardiers or pilots in a B-17 rarely saw the results of their jobs except in pictures. We did.

I have often thought of the second dead German soldier who I saw, propped up against a pine tree, shortly before I was captured. It was obvious he had been mortally wounded and either crawled to prop himself up against the tree or some members of his outfit moved him to the tree. He probably died there alone as the other German soldiers retreated in the face of our company's advance that day. He may have left a wife and children or, if not married, sisters, brothers and parents. An infantryman like myself and perhaps, like myself, fighting for what he believed, never expecting to die.

I'll never forget how it was to feel truly hungry. But no matter how hungry I might be I'll never eat another rutabaga nor the soup made from such. I learned to appreciate our country where those in want are few compared to those who have a bountiful life.

I'll always remember the conversation of one member of Easy Company as he told the Company Commander of a fire fight that had just taken place. He was very excited, gesturing and talking loudly and very fast. It was almost as if he were hyperventilating. Certainly his adrenal glands were at a peak. He told of rounding a corner and found himself facing a German soldier, surprising him. He shot the German soldier before the German had a chance to shoot him. I've often wondered if that member of our Company was bothered in later years because of the events of that day in 1944, in the Vosges Mountains in France.

Some say our generation of eighteen, nineteen and

twenty year old men and women grew up too fast during those war years, and I suppose they are right. It certainly was an accelerated time in our lives and for those around us.

I certainly was not a hero and have no idea would I have been, given the chance. Now, at seventy-five years of age, I'm glad I did not have to kill someone, but I was prepared to do so and would have done so without hesitation. I do have feelings of guilt that I was in a POW camp while the other members of my company helped drive the German Army eastward until their surrender.

A true hero was Maurice Lloyd of Company L of the 399th Regiment, of the 100th Infantry Division, whose body was found in 1976, thirty-one years after he was killed. Lloyd was found in his fox hole near Lemberg, France, still clutching his BAR.

And of course, there was Houston Lee Braly from Brady, the fighter pilot who crashed in France. He was certainly a hero.

Earl Rudder, who headed up the Rangers, was from Brady. Colonel Rudder, another hero, led his troops to scale the bluffs at one of the beaches during the Normandy invasion on June 6, 1944. He later became, in civilian life, the Chancellor of Texas A & M University.

There were many, many heroes in WWII, most of them unsung. I did receive a Bronze Star which I accepted but did not deserve. I was glad I was involved. Despite all of the hardships and loss of life, it was a glorious and heroic era for our country.

As Charles Dickens once wrote, "It was the best of times and the worst of times." It is as if Charles Dickens was speaking of WWII. Mr. Dickens' words do accurately describe my involvement in WWII, although sometimes I think there was more "worse" than "best."

I am glad Hollywood and Steven Spielburg have produced quality and realistic films such as *Saving Private Ryan* and *Schlindler's List* which did not necessarily glamorize war and the era. These needed to be made. I am also glad that Stephen Ambrose and Tom Brokaw published quality books about WWII.

There are many stories told and written by individual members of the armed forces of their involvement in WWII, each unique and different. All should be related and saved in oral or printed form.

This is mine.

A friend of mine, Harry Marlin who lives in Brownwood and is a gifted writer, told me, "Writing a book is an accomplishment itself, and not an easy chore." Harry should know as he has published a few books.

I wanted to go through the whole process; getting the text and graphics as "camera ready," doing the editing, finding a book printer, obtaining an ISBN number and bar code and in general learning as much about book publishing as possible. It has been rewarding and, as Harry said, it is work.

And I have had some wonderful support from friends such as Larry L. King and Ross McSwain (two gifted writers), the members of the West Texas Writers, my nephew Rodney Robinson and my sisters, Dorothy Jean, Betty and Mary Ellen — and many others.

I realize some of the letters I had written home are rather boring for a non-family member to read, but perhaps you, if you are not a family member, will forgive me for not deleting more.

I appreciate the help which was freely given by Donald Cotton, of Cotton Publishing in Lubbock, Texas. I have never met Don, but have visited with him at length on the phone as he informed me of the finer points of getting a book published.

My wife, Nita, has been a great help as she is an excellent editor and very supportive in all matters, including this project.

A.L. (Bud) Lindsey

The web site for the 100th Infantry Division:
www.100thww2.org

The web site for Moosburg, Germany:
www.moosburg.org

The web site for Stanton, Texas
and
The Old Sorehead Gazette magazine
www.stantonfolks.com